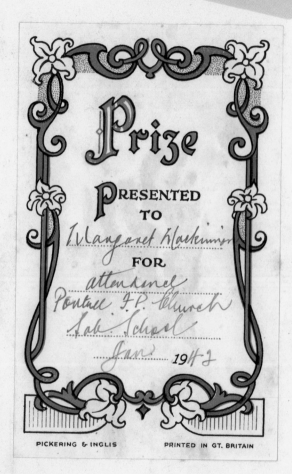

Prize

Presented
To

Margaret Mackinnon

For

attendance

Pontnab F.P. Church

Sab School

Jan 19 4 3

PICKERING & INGLIS   PRINTED IN GT. BRITAIN

THE MISSIONARY
HEROINE OF CALABAR

MARY SLESSOR

THE MISSIONARY
HEROINE of CALABAR

A Story of Mary Slessor

BY

ESTHER E. ENOCK

Author of "Four Girls and a Fortune,"
"F. R. Havergal," etc.

PICKERING & INGLIS LTD.

14 PATERNOSTER ROW, LONDON, E.C.4
229 BOTHWELL STREET, GLASGOW, C.2
EDINBURGH, MANCHESTER, LIVERPOOL, NEWCASTLE.

LONDON - - 14 PATERNOSTER ROW, E.C.4
GLASGOW - - 229 BOTHWELL STREET, C.2
EDINBURGH - 29 GEORGE IV BRIDGE, 1
MANCHESTER 135 DEANSGATE, 3
LIVERPOOL - - 5 HOPE WAY, 8
NEWCASTLE-ON-TYNE 4 CLAYTON STREET.
NEW YORK - LOIZEAUX BROS., 19 WEST 21ST ST.
TORONTO - HOME EVANGEL, 418 CHURCH ST., 2

WE gladly acknowledge our indebtedness to Mr. W. P. LIVINGSTONE, the Author, and to Messrs. Hodder & Stoughton, Ltd., the Publishers of

"MARY SLESSOR OF CALABAR"

for kind permission to draw upon the information contained in their biography, in the preparation of this story.

Made and Printed in Great Britain 94397

Contents

Illustrations

THE MISSIONARY
HEROINE OF CALABAR

CHAPTER I

A Dundee Mill Girl

ONE dark night, outside Wishart Pend, in Dundee, stood a group of rough lads. In their midst was a small, pale-faced girl. The leader of the gang held a piece of lead attached to a string, which he was swinging round her head.

The deadly weapon swung closer and closer with every round, but the girl did not flinch. The boy, as it almost grazed her brow, let the weapon fall to the ground.

" Boys, she's game ! " he cried admiringly ; and a murmur of approval came from each lad there.

" We'll go into your meeting," said the leader, and to the meeting they went. Thenceforth, instead of trying to break up the Mission, they became her staunchest supporters. It was the turning-point in the life of the boy who swung the lead.

And who was this small, brave lassie, who had stood so still and quiet under the ordeal ?

She was Mary Mitchell Slessor, the daughter of a cobbler, and herself a factory hand, but destined by

7

God to be one of His greatest blessings to Africa. Timid enough to be afraid of dogs, but full of courage in the works to which God called her.

She was born in Aberdeen, on December 2, 1848. When first she came to Dundee with her parents and brothers and sisters, she was, as she says, " a wild lassie," and ran about the streets with other children as wild as herself.

An old widow who used to watch these children and felt concern for their souls would often call them into her room and tell them of their need of salvation.

One dark winter afternoon she had gathered them round her fire, and suddenly, with that fire for her text, she showed the children in a few forcible words what is the fate of those who reject God's offer of salvation in the Lord Jesus Christ.

" If ye dinna repent, and believe on the Lord Jesus Christ, your soul will burn in the lowin', bleezin' fire for ever and ever," she said.

No paring down of the awful truth of eternal punishment here, no shaping it to please our weak, shrinking, easy-going nature. These children, young as they were, were in need of salvation ; they were in danger of eternal destruction through neglect of it, and warn them she *must*, and *did*.

Dear, faithful old woman, what a wonderful thing she did for Africa when she spoke those words. Mary Slessor was then and there convinced of her need, and in a little while was rejoicing in the fact that she was saved. " For God so loved the world that He gave His only begotten Son, that whosoever believeth in Him should not perish, but have eternal life."

Henceforth she lived not unto herself, but unto Him who died for her and rose again.

She was able now to be a help and comfort to her mother, who sorely needed it, for Mr. Slessor had fallen into habits of intemperance, which grew worse as time went on. Mrs. Slessor was often reduced to the direst straits in feeding and clothing her children. She, as well as Mary, had to work in the factory, as the father was no support to the home, spending every penny he could get in drink.

Life at the factory where Mary worked for fourteen years, beginning at the early age of eleven years, was very hard. The hours were from 6 a.m. to 6 p.m., with an hour for breakfast and an hour for dinner. She had to be up at 5 every morning in order to help in the work at home, and yet with all these strenuous hours she managed to find time to cultivate her mind; like Livingstone, propping a book up on her loom in order to glance at it in precious leisure moments. On the way to and from the factory her eyes were mostly on her book.

Added to this, she attended the services in Wishart Church, to which her mother belonged; and she had a class of "lovable lassies" in the Sunday school.

When a Mission was started at 6 Queen Street, nearly opposite Quarry Pend, she volunteered as a teacher. This work was attended with dangers, as we have seen, and the older teachers always surrounded the younger ones on leaving the Mission, in order to protect them.

Later on the Mission was transferred to Wishart Pend, where she had charge of classes for boys and girls, both on Sundays and week-nights. It was outside this room the boys had surrounded her when she happened to be alone, on the evening on which our story begins.

The lad who had swung the lead, when he grew to manhood and became prosperous, sent her a photograph of himself, his wife, and family, which photograph decorated the wall of one of her bush houses in Africa.

On another occasion, whilst a very officious young bully, armed with a whip, was pursuing his usual occupation of compelling the lads to go into her meeting, whilst refusing to do so himself, she faced him and asked :

" What would happen if we changed places ? "

" I suppose I'd feel this whip across my back," he replied. Turning her back, she said she'd bear it for him if he'd go in.

" You would really bear that for me ? " the astonished lad asked.

" I would, and much more. So go on. I am in earnest."

But he threw the whip down and went in, and that very night accepted the Lord Jesus Christ as his Saviour.

Wherever Mary Slessor went she exercised a marvellous influence. The rough lads adored her ; the women and children in the darkest, poorest houses where she visited, looked for her eagerly, and many a sad mother was braced and comforted by her courage and cheerfulness. In the factory, the strength and sweetness of her character influenced the workers to such an extent that the whole community seemed to feel it.

Why was it ? How was it ? It was because Mary Slessor's heart was on fire with love and gratitude to Him who had saved her from wrath to come, and her one aim was to bring souls to Him.

Dr. H. Bonar's lines were perfectly exemplified in her life :

" Thou must be true thyself,
    If thou the truth wouldst teach ;
Thy soul must overflow if thou
    Another's soul wouldst reach ;
It needs the overflow of heart
    To give the lips full speech.

Think truly, and thy thoughts
    Shall the world's famine feed ;
Speak truly, and each word of thine
    Shall be a fruitful seed ;
Live truly, and thy life shall be
    A great and noble creed."

Mary seized every opportunity of learning, and the papers she wrote for the Fellowship Association were unusually excellent, showing a happiness in phraseology and a spiritual insight not often found at such an early age. And so, unconsciously, she was being fitted for her life-work, and advancing step by step nearer to the task which was destined for her by God.

In 1874 came news of the Home-call of Dr. Livingstone, and the great wave of missionary enthusiasm which stirred the land set aflame the spark which for years had smouldered in Mary's heart. It blazed up and stirred her to action. She must be a missionary in very truth. She was free from much of the strain of home support now, for Mr. Slessor was dead, and her two remaining sisters in good situations. She herself would be able still to contribute to the maintenance of the home from her salary as a missionary, so she forthwith discussed the matter with her mother.

Mrs. Slessor's heart had always been in the Calabar Mission, and it was through her, humanly speaking, that Mary had become imbued with the desire, so the mother's consent was gladly given. It was a joy to give

Mary, since the two lads whom she had wished to send had both died. Some of Mary's friends were not very enthusiastic over her proposal, but Mr. Logie and Mr. Smith, church members, approved entirely, and Mr. Logie promised to look after Mary's affairs whilst she was abroad. Later he became a member of the Foreign Mission Committee.

Mary offered her services to the Foreign Mission Board of her church—the United Presbyterian—in May 1875, and though her heart was set on Calabar, she expressed her willingness to go anywhere, so eager was she to be sent forth with the life-giving message.

Her offer was accepted, but she was told to continue her studies in Dundee for a time, which she did until December, when the Board, at their own expense, sent her to Edinburgh for special preparation.

On August 5, 1876, at the age of twenty-eight, she sailed for Africa, from Liverpool. Two of her Dundee friends accompanied her to the steamer *Ethiopia*, in which she was to make her voyage ; and the trio, watching some of the cargo put on board, noticed a number of casks of spirit for the West Coast. How often had Mary waged war against such stuff, and how often, during her missionary labours, she would have to do so again. "There are *scores* of casks," she exclaimed, looking at them rather dejectedly; "only *one* missionary!"

But her God could accomplish much with this *one* missionary against the scores of casks, and *did* do so, as this story will show.

The day she landed, September 11, 1876, was the beginning of brighter days for Calabar.

CHAPTER II

The Ways of the People

CALABAR! What scenes the name can bring up before our imagination!

A beautiful land in many parts, but even amidst its beauty lurked disease and sickness, and sin and sorrow. The natives were considered the most degraded in Africa, and small wonder this, taking into account the treatment meted out to them by nations who were more powerful, *and* said to be more civilised than they.

In the fifteenth century the Portuguese opened up the coast and emptied the towns by their slave raids in the same way that the towns on the land side had always been desolated by Egypt and Arabia.

But God can bring good out of evil. Through the conversion of natives from Calabar who had been sold as slaves to Jamaica, the Gospel was sent to their homeland. That had happened thirty years before Mary Slessor came. Mr. Waddell had founded the Calabar Mission in 1846. The Mission stood upon the very hill where the dead bodies of natives used to be thrown to the wild beasts.

Mary was well acquainted with many awful facts relating to the lives of the natives, and the difficulties which she had come to share with the brave souls who had been labouring there already for some time.

Here are a few of those facts, and as you read on through this story you will understand better the terrible and mysterious forces against which missionaries are ranged.

Witchcraft was interwoven with life in such a way as practically to rule the land. Superstition was rife everywhere. When a chief died, numbers of people were murdered, and his wives, after dressing in their finery, were strangled, in order to go with him to the spirit land. Blood sacrifices were offered to jujus; the human skull was worshipped; guilt was decided by poison being administered, or the hands plunged into boiling oil; when twins were born they were always killed, and the mother sent away into the bush to do the best she could, generally to starve and die, or to be killed by wild beasts.

Mary had heard about all these things in far-away Dundee; now she was going to see them for herself, to fight them in the Name of the Lord Jesus Christ, who had died to save these poor degraded people. Saved herself, and overflowing with love to her Saviour, she had a salvation worth speaking about, a real, definite thing; and with this treasure to share with all who would, she went forward eagerly, joyfully, into the dim, mysterious future now opening before her.

It mattered nothing to her that missionaries had been compelled, in speaking of these people, to apply to them some awful names. What these missionaries said was really true; there was no exaggeration. The people were not an attractive people! But this did not move Mary. Did not the Lord Jesus Christ come down to an unattractive, repellent people, and give up His life for them? And should Mary Slessor shrink from any task, however hard and distasteful? Never! She looked upon such tasks as an honour and a privilege to perform.

At the Mission she soon made friends, and fell quickly into Calabar Mission ways. " Mammy " Anderson saw to the latter ; she found that Mary had not left all her love of pranks in Scotland, and the high spirits of the young missionary needed a slight check now and again. There were times when she was late for meals, and the promised punishment of going without food was administered. " Daddy " Anderson, however, probably with " Mammy's " full consent, would convey bananas and biscuits to the offender. " Mammy " Anderson was dearly beloved by Mary.

King Eyo, whose acquaintance she seemed to have made at Creek Town, was a much-valued friend. He was a simple, sincere, kindly Christian, and when Mary told him how much interested Mrs. Slessor was in him, the African king was delighted, and he and Mrs. Slessor used to correspond. So strong a bond is the love of Christ, that it can bridge four thousand miles of sea, between people who have never seen each other.

Then there was Mammy Fuller. She was a coloured woman, and remembered the day when the slaves in the West Indies were emancipated. She never spoke ill of any one. Mary loved Mammy Fuller, and Mammy loved Mary. Little did either of them imagine " dear old Mammy " would live to see Mary laid to rest. But that is many years later. Mary has but just started work in the Mission now.

Her work at first seemed easy. Teaching in the Mission Day School—visiting the compounds weekdays and Sundays. Then, as she began to understand the difficulties of fathoming the native mind, she was sent on a tour among the stations, and in these districts her knowledge of the rough material with which she had to deal increased by leaps and bounds. Mary Slessor's early experiences in the Scottish slums and pends, where she and her companions during open-air work were often pelted with mud—where constant guardianship was needed—helped her now. The courage she had in those earlier days needed to be even stronger, for here she felt herself in contact with evils far more terrible to combat than in the dark places in Aberdeen, Dundee, and Edinburgh.

She had long, tiring journeys from station to station, accompanied by three Kroo boys who were to assist her in arduous climbing and wading—but Miss Slessor's activity and natural buoyancy must have made their task a light one.

A white "Ma" was a new and strange sight to most of the raw natives she visited. Their demonstrations rather alarmed her sometimes, but she was assured it was only friendliness.

Her first address was given in the shadow of a huge tree—a devil-house stocked with food for a dead man's spirit stood near by. John Baillie, a native agent, was with her, and after he had spoken in Efik, he inquired if she would speak to the people. She looked nervously round on the dusky faces, to find every eye upon her. It was a great ordeal, but bravely she undertook it, asking John Baillie to read from the fifth chapter of John's Gospel, verses one to twenty-four—which he did, in Efik. Wonderful indeed must the story have sounded, heard before perhaps, but now to be talked about by this young white "Ma," whom they had never seen before. And as she spoke earnestly, slowly, John acting as interpreter, her heart glowed with love and joy. She spoke of the need of pardon and healing, and finally she put the Saviour's question—" Wilt thou be made whole ? " showing Him as the Way, the Truth, and the Life, reminding them of the promise : " He that heareth My word, and believeth on Him that sent Me, hath everlasting life, and shall not come into condemnation ; but is passed from death unto life."

As time went on she learnt more of the social life of the natives and things which militated against the progress of Christianity. As to the social life—there was the chief, his numerous wives, the numbers of slaves, children, all dwelling in an assembly of mud huts in the forests. Here the chief reigned supreme. The slaves had a certain amount of freedom, but if the chief chose to kill or to sell them he could do so, and none could say him nay. The people in these villages, yards, or compounds, as they were variously designated, were all related, and the chief was absolute ruler. Sometimes this fact was helpful to Miss Slessor in her work, sometimes it was the very reverse, as we shall see when we follow her through the years. At present she is a beginner in Duke Town.

This is an account of the usual Sunday routine. First she sends round illustrated texts to all the big men, with the message that Mr. Anderson is expecting them at the service at four, after which she sets out for the town.

Here is a man rocking himself to and fro at the door of his hut. No, he is not going to service. Why ? " If your heart was sore would you go anywhere at all ? Would you not prefer to stay at home and nurse your grief ? " he asks.

In a moment Mary learns that his only child has died, and the man takes her to his wife, who is weeping over the grave in the hut.

The young missionary reads the story of Lazarus, and the sad, dark hearts are touched at last by the story of resurrection and reunion.

In the next yard she speaks to some slave-girls, who listen quietly. Farther on she has an audience of women, who are lolling on the ground eating, sleeping, or dressing each other's hair. She is a welcome visitor. It is a little diversion, and she is taken to see a young woman who is being fattened for her future husband. Mary has to speak sternly to her, for the message is received contemptuously; the young woman is somewhat crestfallen, though still half defiant when Mary leaves.

After several other visits she comes upon a group of men selling rum. The white " Ma " is such a welcome sight that they put it away and ask her to remain. She talks to them, and for a while they listen, but the moment she speaks against the sale of rum they are angry, and one says :

" Why white man bring them rum, suppose rum be no good ? The God-man bring the rum—then why God-man talk so ? "

Poor missionary ! What can she reply ? She feels very bitter against those god-men (?) who ruin the bodies and souls of their fellow-creatures for the sake of profit. She cannot answer the man.

But " *when* HE *maketh inquisition for blood*," what will these men who have thus profited reply ?

Next she visits a man and his wife who have lost five children. Has she some " medicine " for the sorrowing parents ? She tells again about the resurrection, and the crowd around listens enchanted. Then she says that little twin-children are safe with God, and that they will yet confront those who murdered them. This is awful, and her audience with terror-stricken looks slink away, shrugging their shoulders at the strange and horrible things the white " Ma " has said.

Several more visits of cheer and comfort she pays, and, as the Lord was with her, there was blessing in her train.

Now she repairs to the Mission House for the four o'clock service, tired, but happy.

For nearly three years Miss Slessor laboured, spending herself as we have seen, at Duke Town, but after many attacks of fever, in one of which she nearly died, she was ordered home.

In June 1879 she left Calabar and went to Dundee. During this furlough she moved her mother and sister to Downfield, a village just outside the city.

It was, too, during this furlough that she expressed her desire to go to untouched fields. The pioneering spirit was already at work. But " Daddy " Anderson opposed the idea. She, however, before returning, begged the Foreign Mission Board to send her to a different station, adding at the same time that she would do as they thought best.

She sailed with the Rev. Hugh Goldie and his wife, veteran pioneers in the work, and arrived at Calabar in October 1880. There she heard with deep joy that she was appointed to the charge of Old Town.

CHAPTER III

Light in the Darkness

THE people of Old Town, Qua, Akim, and Ikot Ansa were amongst the most degraded in Calabar. That fact in itself was enough to induce Miss Slessor to go to them.

She was able to pursue her own methods in Old Town, although it was under Duke Town supervision, and, what was very important also, she was able to economise in her way of living in order to leave more of her salary for the dear ones in Scotland, a practice which was not so easy when she was with her colleagues. They did not know this was her reason for preferring to work alone, but put it down to natural inclination, and Mary never enlightened them.

Her house was in a dilapidated condition. It was built of wattle and mud, the roof was formed of mats, and it was whitewashed inside, but repairs were sadly needed.

Mary, however, was too eager and absorbed in her work to pay attention to personal comfort. Her heart must have been on fire with love to the Lord Jesus Christ. To all who came to see her, whether they came in need, or out of curiosity to see what the white woman was like, she talked about the Saviour of the world, and of her visitor's individual need of Him.

On Sundays she was speaking of Him practically from dawn to dark—and after. She used to start early for

Qua, and two boys carrying a bell slung on a pole summoned the people to the meeting. One of the chief men would put the seats ready and settle the congregation, which generally numbered eighty to a hundred.

The meeting over, she would go on to Akim and Ikot Ansa for more, visiting farms and sick folk on the way, giving short addresses and prayers. Back in Old Town by midday for Sunday School; and lastly, *the* service of the week—in the evening.

The yard of the chief was the place of assembly, and nearly every person in the vicinity would be there. A table, covered with a white cloth, a primitive lamp, and the Bible upon it stood in one corner. From there Miss Slessor could see row upon row of dusky faces, those nearest just catching the dim light from the lamp, those farther back merging in the darkness which surrounded them—a strange picture, a touching scene. The light of the lamp might be dim, but the Light of the World was there displayed, and how many souls were brought to acknowledge that Light at these earnest meetings the day of Christ alone will declare.

Against the terrible superstitious cruelties still practised by the natives in spite of laws enacted for their suppression by the Government, Miss Slessor waged incessant war.

Twins were always murdered, because one of them was supposed to be the child of an evil spirit. It was, of course, impossible to tell which of them was of evil origin, and so both must die. They were generally killed and thrust into a calabash, then thrown into the bush. Sometimes they were thrown away alive, to be eaten by insects and wild beasts. It was not permitted that they should be taken out of the hut through the door, but through a hole made in the wall which was hastily refilled.

The mother, herself sharing the superstition, was an outcast, and driven away into the bush, never more to use the native tracks, but to make her own through thorns and over rocks. She considered herself accursed.

Miss Slessor always got hold of any twins the moment it was possible, and some of those she rescued grew up in her house to be a comfort and blessing to her, and a proof to the superstitious folk about her that even twins were precious in the sight of God.

She also used to rescue the babies of slave-women which were thrown away because there was no one to bring them up. Against witchcraft and the poison and burning oil ordeal she never ceased to fight.

Then, too, she tried to introduce a better relationship between the inland and the coast tribes, so that all could reap the benefit of trading—a campaign, this, which won her the hearty approval and sympathy of the traders.

But Miss Slessor was above all things a pioneer. She must *go forward* to preach the salvation that is in Jesus where it had seldom or never been preached. Therefore she used to make tentative excursions up-river, carrying medicine and bandages, and visiting the sick in the riverside villages, telling them at the same time of the Saviour.

At the earnest request of Okon, a chief who lived about thirty miles up the river, she paid his place a visit of a fortnight's duration. Her departure from Old Town created a great deal of excitement for days before she left. Nine a.m. was the time fixed for the start, but Mary knew enough of the ways of her people to go on calmly with her day's work, and at 6 p.m., nine hours later than " scheduled " time, she was summoned to the canoe.

This canoe had been sent by the king, and had a little improvised matting shelter with rice bags for her to rest upon, an act of love and thoughtfulness which touched her heart indeed. Setting her four twin children in the bottom of the boat she waited in patience through further native delays; then, at last, the thirty-three paddles fell into the water and the voyage was begun. There were songs in her honour—one stating that she, their beautiful beloved mother, was on board. And soon the low " tom-tom-tom " of the drum and the gentle motion through the water lulled " Ma " to sleep. In ten hours they reached Okon's place, just as dawn was breaking.

She and the children were given the chief's own room, which looked on to the women's enclosure. All the wives of the chief would sit as close as possible to the white " Ma," making her intolerably warm. There were cheerful little lizards in the matting roof, scattering dust and chips down, whilst now and then a rat would skip past. With one thing and another " Ma " had something to contend with. But—that was why she had come to Africa, and so she set the Lord always before her. To work for Him, to tell of His death for these poor sinners around her, and to win them for Him was all she asked.

Men came from far and near to Okon's to hear her tell " the old, old story of Jesus and His love." And gladly she told it, for she knew it would go from there into many dark and dreary places, shedding light everywhere. It was easy to put up with inconveniences, uncomfortableness, and privations to accomplish that.

There was prescribing, bandaging, cutting out of clothes, lessons in washing, ironing, starching, but dearer than all was the preaching of the Gospel, not to Miss

Slessor only, but to her audience as well. It was the first time many of the people had heard the story, and the numbers who crowded to hear her were so great that her voice could scarcely reach them all. And afterwards those fierce-looking men, some of whom had come through swamps, and dark and difficult tracks for miles, would come up and wish her good-night ere starting on the return journey.

Whilst she was at Okon's a boa-constrictor in the vicinity of the village caused a great commotion. A host of shouting men armed with guns, clubs, and cutlasses started out to hunt it. History does not relate whether they succeeded. Another excitement was a terrific storm which broke over the village, bad enough to make even courageous Miss Slessor afraid. The roof of her hut was swept away amid fearful crashes of thunder and blinding flashes of lightning. The rain was so strong that she was beaten to the ground; but she struggled up again, waded through the deluge to her boxes, and securing all the wraps she possessed, for protection of the little children she had brought with her, rolled the frightened, drenched mites securely up in them at once.

For her, high fever ensued—and knowing how near death always is in Africa, she arranged her affairs in readiness, in case the end should come. But her work was not done yet. Quinine proved efficacious—her temperature went down, and in two days she was all right.

Then came a day when such grave looks were on all faces that she guessed that there was something wrong. There was trouble ahead. Two of the young wives of the chief had wilfully broken Efik law by going into a yard where a boy was sleeping, and the punishment for that offence was one hundred stripes. " Ma " interceded with Okon, and he consented to have a " big palaver." There " Ma " rebuked the girls roundly for their mischievous prank, for it involved two slave-girls as well. Her rebuke excited applause from the men, at which she turned upon them and gave them her frank opinion of their treatment of women, and the system of polygamy, a speech which was *not* applauded.

However, through " Ma's " entreaties, the hundred was reduced to ten and nothing more. In an ordinary way salt would have been rubbed in, and possibly dismemberment or mutilation have followed. She bade the wives and slaves show their gratitude by loyal service, and then she began preparing for relieving the pain of the victims. Their piercing screams were heard above the shouts and laughter of the onlookers as the alligator hide did its work, and, at last, one by one the girls came to her in agony for the comfort and easement she had ready.

At length the return journey to Old Town was taken. Okon himself accompanied her, and on the way they encountered a fearful storm of rain and thunder and lightning, and a wild wind which whirled the frail canoe round, though the rowers were pulling their hardest. The futility of their efforts cowed the crew, and Okon himself gave in to panic. Mary, in the clamour and disorder, took command, and under her God-given calm and self-control the men gained courage again, pulling inshore beneath a tangle of bushes. Leaping into these they hung on to the canoe. Mary sat in it, though it was tossing like a cockle-shell, lashing the children to her with a macintosh, and soothing them with loving words as she always did. Then came a sudden end to the fury of the tornado. The men dropped once more into the canoe and the journey was resumed, the sweet notes of a hymn rising on the night air. But " Ma " was attacked by her old enemy, ague, and was shivering dreadfully. Okon sat one side of her, his large wife the other, to bring some warmth into the poor chilled frame, whilst the rowers pulled as fast as they possibly could. The light of morning was upon them as the canoe beached at Old Town, then Mary was hurried up a bush path to the Mission House. She was very ill by that time, but that did not deter her from first seeing to the needs of the children. After, she fell into her bed. A few days later she was up and about, weak, but with her usual cheerful smile and helpful manner. It was a great relief to see " Ma " like that again.

She was obliged to remove to Duke Town late in 1882 on account of a tornado, which damaged her house so badly that she had to fly from it. In Duke Town she was so ill that the Presbytery ordered her home, and she left in April 1883, taking with her a little girl-twin whom she had saved. The other twin, a boy, had been stolen during one of Miss Slessor's brief absences from her house and killed, therefore she resolved to keep the little girl safely beside her so that she should grow up and show them the folly of their superstition.

On this, her second furlough, Mary was destined to see her dear ones for the last time in this life. Janie, her youngest sister, was very ill, and a change to a warmer climate was imperative. Mary ultimately took a small house in Topsham, and as no other course seemed possible, severed her connection for the time with the Calabar Mission in order to look after her people, hoping that at some future date she would be reinstated. She then went down to Topsham, her salary assured till April.

Shortly came the news of her sister Susan's sudden death, which meant that the entire upkeep of the home devolved upon Mary.

And Mary, by this time, was earning nothing. However, as Janie's health was improving, it became clear that Mary should apply for reinstatement. This was gladly given, and she also had her mother's willing consent to her wish to go up-country on her return to Calabar.

Mary never forgot the courageous assurance from the lips of the woman whose sons had died before they could go to the mission field. This brave daughter had been given to God for His work, and the mother, ill and weak though she was in health, would not stand in the way. " When He needs you and where Hè sends you, there I would have you be," she said.

Everything was arranged for her departure when Mrs. Slessor suddenly failed, and was unable to leave her bed. Mary waited on her Lord for guidance in this sorrow, and shortly a letter was on its way to an old Dundee friend, asking her to come and take charge of the home. That truly noble woman agreed to do so at once, and the devoted missionary was soon on her way across the ocean.

She arrived at Creek Town just before New Year, 1886. Naturally she was anxious about the dear ones she had left behind, little knowing that her mother had reached the heavenly home about the same time that Mary reached Creek Town. In March, Janie died, and the home life was over. Mary turned her face bravely, resolutely, to her work in Calabar.

" Heaven is nearer to me now than Britain, and there

is no one to be anxious about me when I go up-country," she said.

Miss Slessor's next two and a half years in Creek Town were full years. Her household was increasing. First came four-year old Janie, the little girl-twin she had rescued, and who was named after Ma's sister, and baptized in Wishart Sunday School. Then came a girl of six; a boy of eight, Okim, whose new clothes lasted him only about a week; Ekim, ten years old, a son of the king of Old Town, given to Mary Slessor by his mother when the former first went to Calabar. He had gone to his home whilst Mary was in Scotland, but came back to her again on her return from furlough. He was a free boy, and would hold a responsible position some day, so Mary spent much care and thought on his upbringing and training. He, on his part, was affectionate, truthful, and clever. Lastly, there was a big girl of thirteen, Inyang; she was bigger than Miss Slessor, of very low mental powers, but faithful, honest, industrious—a perfect treasure to Mary in the kitchen. She was never happier than when baking and doing housework, and her love and care for the other children was yet another source of comfort.

Besides this household there were other children in the compound—twins who had been found in dark and dangerous places, thrown out to die, and others not wanted by their drunken parents. So we see that family cares were considerable. Added to this was the constant attention given to natives who needed wounds dressed and bandaged, and others who needed medicine. And always, with that ministry, the more important one, the ministry of the Gospel for the salvation of their souls.

Miss Slessor speaks of a dear old blind woman who

lived in Creek Town, whose name was Mary, too. Of her "Ma" Slessor could not speak too highly. Not a penny did she possess except what the Mission was able to give—no one to do anything for her—a ramshackle old home—and yet she was for ever praising the Lord for some new mercy, and giving bright testimony to her precious Saviour. Mary Slessor declared that the old hut was like heaven to more than herself.

CHAPTER IV

Storming a Stronghold

MISS SLESSOR was two and a half years in Creek Town. The last year was occupied largely by negotiations for her removal to Okoyong.

Three times members from the Mission had accompanied her to spy out the land, but were received with sullenness by an armed people. At last, in June of 1888, she resolved to go up again.

King Eyo, of Creek Town, ever her friend, sent her up in his own canoe, fitted out for her in royal state, with Brussels carpet on the floor, a palm-leaf shelter, and a brilliant curtain to screen her from the crew, to say nothing of six pillows on which to rest.

On the way up the river she reviewed the Okoyong situation, which was delicate in the extreme, for her own paddlers were the sworn enemies of the people she was going to visit.

Infinite tact, and love, and patience would be needed. The Okoyong might even be on the war-path. But, like David, she encouraged herself in the Lord her God.

Arrived at the landing beach, she made her way inland four miles to Ekenge, a mud hut village, and was kindly, if noisily, received.

The outcome of this brave visit was a promise from Edem, chief of Ekenge, and also another chief at Ifako, two miles farther, that they would give her land for her missionary enterprise,

She promptly chose the sites, in Ekenge, and at Ifako, two miles farther (these two miles sometimes took thirty minutes to traverse, according to the state of the track). When she made the choice she asked if the buildings, when erected, would be a refuge, like Calabar Mission, for criminals, for unfortunates who were to be slain for the dead, and for twins, and so forth—until each case should be considered. And would the house she intended to build for herself be a refuge also. " Ma," you see, wished to be sure about what she was being given.

To these requests a solemn assent was given to her, for she had captivated them by coming alone.

With this promise she returned to Creek Town, and packed her belongings, amid much shaking of heads and gloomy prophecies from those around, to all of which she only laughed.

King Eyo, good man, came to see to the loading of the canoe, and in the grey, soaking dawn she set off, Mr. Goldie at the last minute sending Mr. Bishop, a member of the missionary staff, with her.

In fading light they landed, and " Ma " immediately started on the four-mile walk through the soaking woods to Ekenge, leaving Mr. Bishop to follow with some of the carriers and dry clothes and necessaries.

" The Lord, He it is that doth go before thee; He will not fail thee nor forsake thee."

Such promises were Mary Slessor's trust as she set out with the four children—first, a boy of eleven, carrying a box on his head filled with tea, sugar, and bread; then a boy of eight, with kettles and pots; after him a boy of three; and lastly a little maiden of five, all more or less tearful. " Ma " walked behind, a bundle on one arm and a baby girl astride her shoulders. She sang funny child songs to cheer the little mites, albeit the tears were in her own eyes. And the rain was streaming down.

A strange little company this, to come to such a stronghold of Satan. But, even so, how weak so e'er the instrument, in God's hand it is mighty.

There was no one at home at Ekenge when the little party arrived, except some slaves. Every one was at Ifako for the carnival on the occasion of the death of the chief's mother. She had died that morning.

A fire and water were soon ready, and the children undressed and asleep, and " Ma " awaited Mr. Bishop's arrival with the carriers. He came at last and informed her that the men refused to bring anything up that night.

What was to be done ! " Ma " looked round at the cheerful fire, the singing kettle. To-morrow, Sunday, nothing could be brought up. There was nothing to eat. Prompt action was needed. She asked Mr. Bishop to collect some slaves. They were to be sent after her to carry things—she was off again herself—but would not the boy just dispatched to the beach with the stern message, and his lantern, be of any avail ? No—the men would take no notice—*she must go*—and go she did, hatless and bootless. It was a fearsome walk—one ray of pleasure came with the hurrying footsteps of one of the boys from the village to keep her company. So dark was it that his white clothes were hardly visible at times —they fell along rather than walked, and the shouts of the slaves behind, who were making a commotion in order to keep beasts of prey at a distance, sounded weird in the strange blackness which was around. Now and again she heard the flapping of the night-birds' wings, the

"WE'LL GO INTO YOUR MEETING," SAID THE LEADER
AND TO THE MEETING THEY WENT   (Page 7)

To face page 32

"FOR WHILE WE SMILE ANOTHER SMILES,
AND SMILES COME QUICK IN PILES AND PILES!"

rapid movements of slinking things, saw the fire-fly's light here and there, and felt the touch of branches on her cheek. Presently the lad with the lantern came shouting up to them. The men had refused to move, as she knew they would.

The party hurried on, and soon Miss Slessor has reached the water—the canoe is under her hand—the tarpaulin which covers the sleeping crew suddenly whirls off them, and they sit up astounded, and ashamed. " Ma " was adept in managing, and in a minute the whole crowd were working as hard as they were able. Before midnight, all that she needed for the nonce was safely housed at Ekenge.

The next day, Sunday, August 5, 1888, her first in Okoyong, was one of the saddest she ever spent, partly, no doubt, on account of her extreme weariness after the strenuous hours of Saturday. She managed to have a little service with the women who returned—some with fractious babies, some for more food for the orgy at Ifako—and her heart was somewhat cheered.

Miss Slessor spent fifteen years in Okoyong. The sadness of that first Sunday was amply compensated for as the years went by. The fifteen years showed marvellous results and a great harvest of souls.

But at what a cost ! " Ma " had to be on the qui vive practically night and day, ready at a moment's notice for any emergency—" Run, Ma, run ! " and off she would go, either to the rescue of twins, or to some palaver or poison ordeal, and what not.

But, to return—at the moment she has her temporary home to fit up, and the fact that the villagers are at Ifako made her task easier. The room set apart for her use was in the women's enclosure of Edem's harem. Edem was the name of the chief of Ekenge, you remember. This room was very dirty, but Mary soon got it into a clean and fairly pleasant state. She had the door which had been brought from Creek Town put in at one end, and the window-frame fitted into the wall—a mud wall—then she filled in the holes and spaces around the frame with mud. Next, she cleared a part of the ground allotted to her and fenced it round. In the comparative seclusion thus afforded she was able to do her washing. One can imagine the satisfaction with which she would survey the results of her labours.

Her spiritual work soon began. A tiny orphan was brought to her. It was so poorly nourished that it looked hardly human, and caused much amusement among the natives in the enclosure. The father had been killed in a fight between Okoyong and Calabar—beheaded. The mother had never recovered the shock, and the poor little unwanted baby girl was brought to the white " Ma." Miss Slessor nursed and tended it with great care, to the great entertainment of the onlookers, with the exception of the old grandmother, who blessed Mary for her goodness. The mite rallied for a time under her treatment, but eventually faded away like a withered flower. As a rule no care was taken in the disposal of the body of an infant or a child, but Miss Slessor did not intend to follow native custom. The little thing was dressed in white by her loving hands, a coffin was made out of a provision box, and flowers were placed upon it. Then a native bore the light burden to a spot which Mary pointed out in her ground, a grave was dug, and the strange white woman stood there and prayed, the old grandmother weeping at her side. The revelling crowd at Ifako had got wind of these doings, and rushed over to be present. Now they stood at a little distance—outwardly scornful, inwardly intensely curious. This white woman who had come to live among them was indeed behaving unusually. What a waste of the box, and what a waste of a white robe ! Things had come to a pass indeed, if this sort of thing was going to be done frequently.

Later on, when the whole population of Ekenge was once more at home, they seized a boy who had remained in the village during part of the Ifako celebrations, and who had been doing what he could for Miss Slessor. He was punished for his absence by having burning oil poured over his hands. Mary saw what was going on too late to stop it. She suffered almost as much as the poor lad, but she realised afterwards that even if she had interfered it would not have been wise at this early stage of her residence amongst them. They were following their custom—a law of their tribe—she would have to teach them gradually how evil such things were. But her heart felt sore at the cruelty and superstition she saw all around, and which would take such years to change or quell, so age-long and deep-rooted was it.

Shortly after this incident the people went off again to take vengeance on a neighbouring family of mourners, and there was a week of fighting and turmoil. No sooner had they returned than the death of a freeman called them away again. Mary took the opportunity of making the women appreciate her presence among them. There were many things she was able to do to win her way into their hearts, and she tended the sick folk as well as the children, and as a consequence her foothold at Ekenge was becoming firmer every day.

When the usual routine of daily life was once more

resumed at Ekenge, Mary Slessor realised what she was up against. There was in the village a newly bought slave-wife of Edem's. Mary saw her, sullen and fierce, plastering with mud the sides of a house intended for a freeborn wife, and spoke a few kind words to her as she passed. No doubt, knowing the ways of the natives, Mary may have wondered where the fierce and brooding thoughts would lead the poor young woman. She was soon to know. The girl went to one of the farms belonging to Edem, her master, and sat down in a slave's hut. The poor slave knew well what would follow; the girl was wreaking a subtle vengeance on her master and his relatives, and this slave would suffer for the girl's pretended association with himself. He hurried away at once to his work. The girl went off into the forest and hanged herself. The slave was taken prisoner next day and brought to court in irons. Edem and his relatives were furious at having been associated with a common slave such as this man was, and they decided that he must die.

Miss Slessor was present at the trial, and cried out at the injustice. What wrong had the man done? she asked. Was it his fault that the girl had sat down in his hut? The men replied that the slave must have put the idea in her mind by sorcery, and in any case the witch-doctor had said he was guilty. When Miss Slessor persisted the crowd got very angry. Why should a stranger, there on sufferance, try to thwart the actions of a freeborn people? The prisoner must die. Threats were shouted, weapons of all kinds were waved, but Miss Slessor, "stayed upon her God," stood quietly amidst it all. At last the fury cooled down, and after another palaver they said the man should not die. He was merely starved, flogged, and his chained body cruelly hacked about to rid him of the sorcery within. But Mary had conquered.

Edem, the chief of Ekenge, had a sister called Ma Eme, a widow of a chief. Ma Eme was Mary's firm friend and ally, and secretly kept her well informed of all the concealed, dark doings of the people, often at risk of her own life. She was a great big woman, always acting as peacemaker and intercessor between her brother and his wives. Mary noticed some marks on Ma Eme's arm, and pointed out her own vaccination marks. Ma Eme calmly said : " These are the marks of my husband's teeth."

When Mary arrived at Ekenge, Ma Eme had just returned from her husband's funeral celebrations, at which she had been subjected to a fearful ordeal because she, in common with all his wives, had come under suspicion of having brought his end about by sorcery. Ma Eme, big, strong, self-controlled woman though she was, had fainted outright on being pronounced not guilty by the witch-doctor. The strain had been too much for her.

She was quite casual in her way of telling Mary what caused the marks on her arm. It was nothing. No one could prevent a man biting his freeborn wife, beating her nearly to death—or killing her, if the fancy took him. It was wonderful that this woman was such a sterling character. Her care of Mary, the way she brought her food, and looked to it that the white " Ma " should be as comfortable as was possible in those wilds, and amid such untaught people, was all done with the grace of a high-born lady. She would be careful to speak to Miss Slessor in a softened and refined tone, and in her presence to behave with true refinement. She must have been a great solace to Mary, and the help she gave her by keeping her posted in all the latest information must have been invaluable.

For the first few weeks of her sojourn in Ekenge, Mary Slessor had to live in the harem, the memory of which never left her. Some of the horrors she witnessed are not to be described. " Had I not felt my Saviour near me I should have lost my reason," she said.

But in that place she learnt some valuable lessons— yes, though the memory of those weeks would call hot flushes to her cheek, and make her wince with shame— lessons about the poor women amongst whom she sought to spread the Gospel, lessons about the little children whom she loved, and the troublesome older ones whom she found it hard to love sometimes.

Her room was next to that of Edem and his chief wife. Five other wives were not far off; in the enclosure were slaves, visitors, and children, and animals, insects, cats, rats, and various other specimens of wild life. At night she erected a screen of boxes, behind which the three boys slept; at the other side of this she and the two little girls slept. All other belongings were placed outside for the hours of rest, in order to make room for her and her family. Generally the things required drying in the day after a rainy night. In these queer quarters Mary Slessor solaced herself with her Bible, prayer, and hallowed thoughts of other days, as preparation for each present one.

In the daytime the quarrelling between the wives was trying. Also the custom of keeping this white visitor continually in their company. " Ma " longed unspeakably for quiet and solitude ; she wanted to get away by herself to hold communion with her Heavenly Father ;

to pour out her heart before the Lord. When the longing became unbearable she would slip off to her piece of ground, hoping for solitude and peace ; but, alas ! in sheer politeness to the visitor the others would follow, and poor Miss Slessor would start hacking at the bush with a machete, making such a noise that the voice of her prayer was lost in it. But those ears, ever open to our prayers, heard her, and her prayers were answered.

And these poor wives, they had less liberty than the lowest slaves in reality. Unwritten law hedged them in, and the breaking of that law brought dire vengeance. Often they were unwittingly broken, or forced to do so. Of this last here is a case in point. A man was employed by a girl-wife. The man's master sent for him, and the man before he left asked the girl for the food which was due to him, being part of his hire. To do this was against harem law, and the girl refused, because her husband was not there. When the man persisted she gave him a piece of yam. This infringement of harem law soon became known, and the poor girl-wife found herself bound and sentenced to a trial by ordeal of burning oil. When the punishment began, Mary heard her screams and raced to the spot, and pleaded eloquently for the victim. There was the usual noisy refusal and clamour, but " Ma " won ; she soon had the young girl on her verandah, and felt happy, despite the fact that the captive was in chains till dawn.

From her harem days Mary Slessor learnt that the African women, whilst presenting a hard and callous exterior, the result of age-long oppression and brutal treatment at the hands of man, could be as tender and affectionate as a white woman. In many instances they would venture almost life itself to do a kindness. Mary saw this well exemplified. A number of prisoners, some of them mothers with babies in arms, lying on the ground in chains, waiting the ordeal by poison bean, and nearly fainting with thirst, suffering all the tortures of suspense and terror through a long hot day, awoke the pity of the village women, and not all the fear of unwritten law could deter the older ones from stealing out with water when the guard left for a time at dusk. To the children first, then the mothers, then came some cooked rice from Mary. She had anticipated the chance and was ready; the women took it to the prisoners. They would have been killed had they been found out.

So Mary rejoiced to find these poor degraded women had within them such Divine compassion, and it made her hopeful of teaching them to train and care for their children better. It shocked her unspeakably to see the little ones given intoxicating drink to make entertainment for their elders. The poor ignorant, down-trodden women never attempted to discipline their children. Mary visioned a time when all this would be different. The knowledge of the Saviour would help them to tread a higher path, and from her close contact with these dusky sisters she learnt where and how to serve them best.

Lying was rife among the children. For the slave-children there was some excuse, for they could live only by stealing and lying. Often deceitfulness was their only means of pleasing. No wonder Miss Slessor's gentle heart ached for them. She started a school for these little ones as soon as possible, and songs about the Saviour floated under the trees where hitherto only songs of war and hatred had been heard. The verandah of a house served as schoolroom at first, logs were the seats,

and for lesson books there was an alphabet card attached
to one of the posts ; and over and above they learnt by
word of mouth to chant the simple creed that Jesus the
Son of God came down to earth to save us from our sins,
ending with the wonderful truth that He has returned to
heaven to prepare a place for us.

Sometimes the pupils were not all children, but the
elders soon dropped off and returned to work.   The
attendance was good, though remaining at thirty, and
the singing, which came after spelling, was so enjoyable
that it kept Miss Slessor very late.

These doings were soon bruited abroad, and chiefs
from other districts wanted Miss Slessor to come to them
and teach.   There were some who were called " The
Terror of Calabar."   These came in person to prefer
their request that she would visit them, and to prove
their peaceable intentions laid down their arms before
speaking to her.   Mary felt tempted, but Edem, her own
chief, warned her against the move, advising her to wait
a while.

It seems as though Miss Slessor quietly acquiesced, for
no doubt he did not wish her to run into any danger, and
he, if any one, should know.   So Mary just carried on
with her schools at Ifako and Ekenge, and held services
too, as usual.

But one day she was summoned to her chief's private
room.   There, with Edem and Ma Eme, she found
messengers from a village near Cross River, eight hours'
journey distant from Ekenge.   They had a tale to tell.
Their chief was at death's door, and they had been visited
by the wife of a chief near by who had told them of Mary,
the wonderful white " Ma " who had saved her own
grandchild and many others.   She would cure the chief.

Forthwith messengers were dispatched with a small and curious gift—four rods and a bottle—would she come at once?

She decided to go, but Edem endeavoured to deter her. It was a long journey and dangerous, and Ma Eme spoke of the deep streams she would have to cross—of deluges of rain. " Ma " was unmoved. Edem, on this, ordered the messengers to return and send an escort of armed men and freewomen. Well he knew the necessity for this, but eager Miss Slessor feared he was only putting hindrances in her path till it should be too late. In this she misjudged him.

With the morning came the escort of freewomen. The armed men, they said, would join them outside the village. Rain was pelting down, and throughout the long walk seemed ever to increase in violence, and Mary's clothes becoming too heavy with the weight of water, she had to discard most of them by degrees. Trudging across a market-place through crowds of natives she felt overwhelmed with shame at her appearance, and wondered if these natives would ever respect her again. Little did she know the effect her coming as she did was to have ! On they struggled, and here is a place where the chief is anything but pleasant to Mary. However, they got through at length, and reached the dying chief's home. Before the door were fierce men ready to slay those who were to accompany him to the spirit-land. Sometimes the " retinue " would number over forty. Mary knew if she could cure the sick man she would save many lives; some of those woebegone-faced women would smile again. She went in at once, not waiting to change her soaking garments until she had done all she could for him at the moment. This over, she left him and donned the clothes the women had piled up for her till her own should be fit for wear. She shuddered as she put them on, but after all what a trifle that, if the man's life was saved! She then went out to find a messenger. More medicine was needed, and to go to Ekenge for it was impossible. There was a quicker method of obtaining it. She inquired if there was a road to Ikorofiong, and was told that a road led to the river, and doubtless a canoe would cross, but they themselves would be killed if they went. Well, she must have some one who would go to Mr. and Mrs. Cruickshank at Ikorofiong for medicine; and then she was told that a Calabar man, son of an Okoyong woman, lived in his canoe quite near. Down to the river, and when the man, whose canoe was off-shore for safety, found that a white woman needed it, he came at once. In as short a time as possible he made the journey, bringing back not only medicine but tea, sugar, various other comforts, and, most delightful, a letter filled with cheering words and encouraging thoughts. Mary knew that she had friends quite near her, and her heart felt light and warm.

Her care and devotion to her patient had the blessed result of bringing him back out of the shadow of death. Consciousness returned, strength began to be renewed, and all who had so feared his passing now breathed freely. The women helped her in a reliable way with the nursing, and there was no more waiting about to slaughter an escort. The chief would live, as Mary would tell herself, by the great mercy of God.

On the recovery of their chief all the village changed in attitude. There was a vision of peace. They would make friends with Calabar, they would like to trade, and best of all they would like to learn " book." Mary answered questions by the hundred, she also held services every morning and evening, and her audience was one of the most reverent she had had anywhere.

But the day of departure arrived. She was sorry to go, and they—how they grieved to let her go! She promised that she would always be their mother, and would come and see them again. And she would try to send them a teacher.

We could imagine she would ask herself on the journey back to Ekenge had it been worth while—the drenching walk—the hard sick-nursing? Yes, indeed! She would recall that last night at Ekenge when she awaited her escort of freewomen. How fiercely doubt had assailed her! But assurance that she had made the right decision had come before dawn, and she said triumphantly:

> " Fear not, ye saints, fresh courage take!
>   The clouds ye so much dread
>   Are big with mercy, and shall break
>   In blessings on your head."

And so it had proved, for her courage, bravery, and skill had made Okoyong free to her thenceforward.

Against sorcery and witch-doctors " Ma " had to fight continuously.

When her own chief, Edem, was ill, she attended him at first, but one morning there was evidence of the witch-doctor in the form of a parcel of shot, powder, teeth, bones, seeds, egg-shells, and all sorts! All these, it was asserted, had been taken out of Edem's back (he was suffering from an abscess in his back), and, of course, as some one was to blame for this state of things, people were being denounced by the witch-doctor and seized.

Mary's remonstrances so angered the chief that he had himself and his prisoners conveyed to his farm, where she could not follow. Presently she heard that the prisoners were to die, as Edem was growing worse. But one night a deputation came to her for a letter to the native pastor at Adiabo, to ask him to see what his skill would do. She gave the letter at once.

The native pastor, however, when told that the soul of some one was troubling the chief, refused to go. His sister went as nurse, and under her care the abscess broke—the prisoners were released, except one woman, who was put to death.

Here is another case of " sorcery."

A chief came to visit Edem, and as a matter of course there was fearful drinking. On the day of their return to their own village, they were so intoxicated that " Ma " accompanied them as protection for the villages they passed through. On the way a plantain sucker was discovered in the path, with a few palm leaves and nuts, a sight which made the brawling natives fly in terror ! Back must they go to the last town they had passed and wreak vengeance for this " sorcery " laid in their path. But " Ma " barred the way, and dared them to go back. In the end they went on homewards by a long detour. " Ma " laughingly pitched the rubbish into the bush, but kept the plantain sucker to plant in her own yard.

Next morning the chief she had accompanied sent for it, with information that (the usual articles apparently) teeth, shot, hair, seeds, fishbones, etc., had been taken out of his leg by the native doctor. Some one was to blame. The plantain sucker was for evidence.

Of course Miss Slessor had to give it up to the messengers, and Chief Edem remarked that it meant that some one would die.

There was a perfect orgy of ordeals in the villages accused, and a man's life-blood was demanded in settlement. The villages, knowing their innocence, stood out against it, but in spite of the stout resistance a young man was taken by the chief's tools and hidden away. It would not have been wise to try to rescue him, for had this been done, murder would have followed. The young man's life would be forfeit in any case. Into the sorrow and perplexity came the thought of the white " Ma," and immediately messengers were sent to beg her to come and plead for the prisoner.

Miss Slessor consented, but never had she disliked a task so much. The chief was a callous, detestable brute, and it was with shaking knees that she came into his presence. He guffawed and chuckled at her entreaties, and when she very clearly pointed out that, since every ordeal and oath the law demanded had been taken, his action was most unjust. He then informed her that it was due to her presence he had escaped death, but nevertheless the people had murdered him in intention. Offensively the head-wife took sides with him, and both walked out of the house as Mary would not. He announced his intention of visiting his farm. Mary followed, humbly begging him to set the prisoner free. He only laughed, and showed his pleasure in her humble attitude.

She returned home. Edem was very angry at the arrogant behaviour of the man, and it looked as though the affair might end in bloodshed. Those days of strain were like a nightmare to Mary. She made her days one continuous prayer. " Is thy God, in whom thou trusteth, able to deliver? " Edem wondered, doubtless, as he and Ma Eme watched the white " Ma."

One morning came news ; news, good and bad, travels

fast in the bush, and this morning it came on wings of joy. The young man had been set free, without any bargaining or reason given, and sent home to his people.

The sense of relief, of peace which followed, is indescribable. There would be no fight now, the fast-ripening quarrel between the brutal chief and Edem came to an abrupt end.

" Ma's " heart was full of praise.

CHAPTER V

Triumphs in Okoyong

THE natives were lolling about in the village, propping the trees up with their brawny backs, and discussing " Ma " and her unseemly haste about the building of her house. Why hurry? A year or so, that was surely time enough to begin to think about getting the materials together. Once they made a start, well— you would see how they could work; but this hurry of Ma's—pah! And so they settled themselves more comfortably against the tree trunk, or on the ground, sprawling full length in luxurious idleness—unhurriedness.

" Ma," therefore, after futile efforts to clear the ground and extract the roots herself, returned to her domestic and pastoral duties, tending the sick, entertaining visitors, acting as general rag-mender to the community, cutting out garments for those whose desires lay in that direction, and caring for her household of little ones.

Then all at once a spirit of industry and vigour pervaded the village. Miss Slessor's ground was invaded by excited natives; tree trunks, bamboos, and all the impedimenta needed for her house appeared as if my magic, and " Ma " found herself surveyor, architect, and foreman all at once.

Four tree trunks were carefully sunk into the ground. These had either a branch fork or were artificially forked to take horizontal logs, then the space was filled in with interlaced bamboos, the whole covered with palm

SUDDENLY ANOTHER CANOE SHOT OUT ACROSS THE RIVER AND
COLLIDED, QUITE POLITELY, WITH HERS   (Page 81)

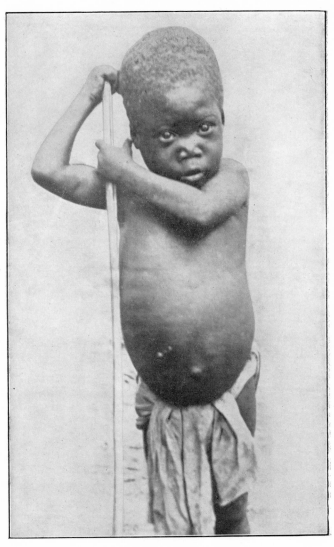

"SUFFER LITTLE CHILDREN, AND FORBID THEM NOT, TO COME UNTO ME: FOR OF SUCH IS THE KINGDOM OF HEAVEN" (Matt. 19. 14).

mats. In front the roof projected to form the verandah top. Round the sides stakes were driven in, other thinner stakes were interlaced, covered with red clay to make a solid wall, and there you are ! She had two rooms, each measuring eleven feet by six. At the outside a shed was built at each end, forming a three-sided square. Fires were lighted, burning night and day to kill insects and protect the place against vermin, as well as to dry it. Next came the digging of the drains and the clearing of the bush. Bush must not be close to any dwelling in African forests ; it is dangerous—a place where evil might lurk unperceived—Mary always kept it down. " Keep thine heart with all diligence."

Now for the inside. Miss Slessor furnished it largely with red clay furniture. There was a sideboard, a dresser ; places were cut and polished to hold bowls, cups, etc. ; the top had a ledge to prevent plates from slipping off, and the whole given a fine black polish of native composition. She made a clay sofa, very necessary for resting her poor tired body occasionally—very occasionally, I fear. Beside the red clay fireplace was a clay seat for the convenience of the cook. The other room took boxes, sewing-machine (rusty with long exposure), some furniture, and an organ, which last had to stand on the bed during the day.

Miss Slessor very aptly dubbed this residence her " caravan." All her cooking utensils hung on the posts, as did her reading sheets and alphabet cards, for of course any casual visitor should be able to do a little learning of " book " in passing. And they passed pretty often, and stood still to admire, for never had such a marvellous dwelling been erected ; they gazed upon it with rapture and awe. And most of

4

the village cattle appreciated the space between the sheds.

Mary loved it. She and her " family " had the merriest meals there, all round one pot, and felt they had never enjoyed food so much before.

And now, the next thing was church and school. These were to be built at Ifako, for then she would have control of a bigger territory. But the native superfluous energy having exhausted itself in the erection of the " caravan," neither chief nor people evinced any interest, and Miss Slessor carried on her village and domestic work in dogged patience. Some day—she told herself.

And, yes, it came at last. A boy from Ifako appeared one morning, briefly informing her that his master wanted her. Not one of the most polite messages, and, rather wondering what it meant, Mary went at once ; two miles over very doubtful tracks.

But when she arrived, all troubled surmisings and forebodings vanished. A crowd of smiling natives were assembled, bright eyes in dusky faces watching her eagerly, the chief waiting in smiling welcome, too. And they were assembled on the ground which had been given her for her buildings ; the place was entirely clear of bush and roots, and all the materials were there—tree trunks, stakes, clay, and a band of willing workers. Mary planned the hall. It measured thirty feet by twenty-five, and at the end were two rooms as a refuge for herself when palaver, storm, or anything else made it impossible for her to return home. The building began at once. It was all to be done only by free people, no slaves were to help. Irresistibly the words come to mind : " Ye must be born again " ; then follows : " Ye also, as lively stones, are built up, a spiritual house . . . acceptable to God by Jesus Christ."

Thousands of palm mats were used for the roof. King Eyo of Creek Town sent those by water, and they were carried by freewomen by way of that very four-mile track along which Miss Slessor had trudged with her " family " that night of her arrival to settle in Ekenge. Freewomen plastered the walls, flattened the floor, and lastly (very important), cleaned up the mess, and all for the love of it. The doors and windows were to be fitted by a carpenter from Calabar, when he could be procured, of which, more anon.

And that was how the first building for the worship of God was raised in Okoyong.

After this, of course, would come the opening, and for that Mary had planned, and stored, for months. What she had stored was now brought out of the Mission boxes—garments, many of them made in England, which were put on to the little children, after they had been well bathed. Like a lot of dusky butterflies they must have appeared in those dresses of many shapes and colours. And it was the first time they had been arrayed in clothes of that kind. " The wearing of a garment always brings self-respect ! " said Miss Slessor, and certainly the assembly gathered for the ceremony was very joyous and clean, and all arrayed in Sunday attire, which in some cases was only a freshly washed skin, and attended to the service with a reverence and gladness that most surely was an earnest of still better things.

The chiefs were present, and solemnly ratified the promise given to Miss Slessor on the occasion of her choice of ground. The building was solely for the service of God. Instruction would there be given to children and slave-women—weapons should not be allowed in it—and for all who fled to it for sanctuary, as such it should be faithfully regarded. We can imagine how happy Miss Slessor felt !

At Ekenge she intended to have a larger Mission House. It was to be in front of the enclosure, there, and would be a more difficult undertaking. The erection of that was deferred for a while.

This gave Miss Slessor time to carry out an idea she had had in mind for some time. It was that, if the people could be interested in trading in something other than drink—the curse alike of the whole community—they would have less time and inclination for drink. Many a night had she gone to bed well aware that not one man and but few women for miles around were sober. Many a time had the revellers from some distant drunken orgy wakened her and asked how it was she had not been waiting their return ! They would make themselves drunk any hour, and after falling about would fall asleep for as long as the spirit, rum mostly, exercised power. She longed to change this. Success had attended her to the extent of prevailing on the chiefs not to drink during " palaver." The improvement was soon apparent, for the distant members went home steadily, and without fighting. Idleness and isolation and the ease with which rum was obtained, Miss Slessor reasoned, was the root-cause of drunkenness. If only she could get these people to be friendly with Calabar ! But they had sentries everywhere, and every missionary who came to see Mary was stopped, and not till the sentry was satisfied and coo-ed to the next was the visitor allowed to proceed. Such was the aloofness of Miss Slessor's people. She started her trading mission by showing off her own things—organ, sewing-machine, meat-safe, curtains, bedstead, and all the things dear to a woman's heart—as far as she could. The men were much intrigued by her window and door, and more than one thought to have one, even if he made it. Then the dress material—that appealed to her dusky sisters, and for all who wished it, she cut out long, straight, simple dresses. And how nice they looked in them !

But this strategy was not enough. She sent to Calabar and begged some native traders with whom she was acquainted to bring in household utensils, dress-stuffs, and any other useful things, telling that she could promise protection. But the Okoyong warriors were so feared that the proposal was firmly declined. So Mary Slessor, not easy to beat, asked King Eyo, her fast friend, to invite some of her people down to palaver. She felt confident of his reply, for he had never ceased his practice of sending messengers to ask if there was anything he could do for her, or for the Okoyong people, and for the replies to be brought back to him by the same messengers. His grandson, too, had often sent men to do anything they could for her. King Eyo at once sent the invitation, and every chief in Miss Slessor's vicinity decided to accept. First the canoe, then gifts in the form of yams and plantains for the king; for trading purposes there were bags of palm kernels and a barrel of oil. The first canoe was swamped through ignorance in lading; the second was managed better, but several chiefs disappeared; more stood on the bank—two only embarked when the order to leave arms behind was issued by " Ma." She was inexorable. For two hours she sat there, waiting, and it was not till after two hours' palaver that guns and swords were passed over to the women. The chiefs and men who refused to go were received with affection, those who were going were bidden wailing farewells. They would never, never return ! And now for a start at last. Ah ! how badly balanced is the canoe. Those bags must be moved. Ma watched anxiously, no further upset required. But what is that gleam ? Swords, swords secreted beneath the bags of kernels. With flashing eyes Ma rose, and grasping the weapons sends them flying back on to the beach, scattering the crowds there gathered as if they were flying from bombs. No outcry or protest this time. Meek and mild rowers take their seats ; " Ma " takes hers, handling her paddle as well as any, in spite of her recent exertions. In black darkness, and a steady drizzle, the canoe sped down-river for twelve hours.

Calabar, Creek Town, and King Eyo waiting to receive " Ma " and to treat her like a queen. A true Christian gentleman, he showed the greatest courtesy to his rather bombastic and flamboyant visitors, evidently for the sake of the white " Ma," of whom he thought the world. At the arbitration conference, or palaver, which had been a very important object of the expedition, he let the Okoyong chiefs state their grievances against the lofty Calabar chiefs (his people), and in a quiet speech he showed the latter that theirs was the greater responsibility. Christianity had been among them a long time, and made them what they were. But they were not all they should be ; they should remember that the Okoyong had but recently come into contact with Christianity. In the quarrel, he judged the verdict went against the Calabar chiefs ; according to the righteousness of God, he gently told them. And so the palaver ended amicably, and the chiefs were entertained at King Eyo's palace. Next day he invited them all to a meeting in the church, speaking sweet words of cheer and loving counsel from the text : " To give light to them that sit in darkness and in the shadow of death, to guide our feet into the way of peace." Can you picture the church, and the crowd of dusky warriors listening to the old native king, as he read and spoke on those sacred words prophetically uttered by the aged Zacharias ? Surely the Dayspring from on high visited Creek Town.

A great impression was made upon the turbulent chiefs. Profound reverence for the king was there, and one and all they determined to yield to his decisions in all disputes in the future. And there was also increased respect for the white " Ma." She evidently was a person of importance, and henceforth must be treated as such. This resolution was put into practice the day after the return of the expedition to Ekenge. A fearful hubbub awakened Miss Slessor. She looked out in astonishment at a crowded yard. Chiefs were there directing slaves, who were very busy with stakes and clay. She asked what was the matter, but instead of giving her a direct answer, a chief who had been one of the expedition addressed the crowd, telling them of Creek Town, of European mode of living—how King Eyo and all the chiefs had given to their Mother more honour than to any one. Okoyong people must do the same. They must build her a house which was worthy of one in so high a position, and so on. Mary withdrew with a smile. During the day a young man, between whom and the whip Mary had often stood, had the temerity to try to wash his hands in a bowl of " Ma's," and it was all she could do to prevent his master from lashing him for the impertinence !

But Miss Slessor had succeeded in her wish. Trade

in good things was started, and friendly relations, with Calabar. Oil making, produce packing, journeys to and fro, filled up the time once spent in idleness and folly. " Satan finds some mischief still for idle hands to do " is very true in Africa as elsewhere. And there was far less senseless palavering, far less drinking, and, thank God, fewer quarrels. That all would be smooth sailing she knew was impossible, but great progress had been made. She felt thankful for the mercies vouchsafed.

CHAPTER VI

Still Christ Triumphs in Okoyong

IN far-away Edinburgh a carpenter named Charles
Ovens was paying a farewell visit to an old lady,
one of his friends, before starting on his return
voyage to America. His baggage was packed and
addressed.

Said the old lady to him : " America again ? Miss
Slessor is needing a good carpenter, a Christian man, to
put in the windows and doors of that hall just built
by the natives. Why not you ? "

Mr. Charles Ovens had wanted to be a missionary, but
had an impression that only ministers could fill such a
post, and the suggestion that he go out was rather a
surprise. Was it possible that he could after all do more
definite missionary work than just putting his hand in his
pocket ? Discussing the matter, and learning all about
Miss Slessor and her labours in Okoyong (there was an
account in the March 1899 *Missionary Record* of the
opening minus doors and windows), this " Scot of Scots "
promptly answered an advertisement in that paper for
a practical Christian carpenter for Calabar. He was
gladly accepted—altered the address on his luggage
labels, and started for Africa.

When he arrived at the Mission House from Duke
Town, Mary jumped up from a table in the yard where
she was surrounded by children, goats, and fowls, her
heart thrilled at the familiar Scots tongue. He was of the

greatest help and comfort during his stay. Her " up-
stairs " at the Mission showed his skill, and he worked
with songs and laughter on his lips. Windows and doors
presented no difficulty to him, much to the awe of the
natives, and for a time the work went on apace. But
always, in Africa, things could happen which led to many
other dreadful happenings, and weeks were often spent
in quelling riots and preventing bloodshed following on
accidents for which no one was to blame.

And thus it came about one lovely morning, when
Mary was happily watching Mr. Ovens at work on the
new house. She lifted her head and listened intently.
Mr. Ovens paused, hammer in hand. A strange sound
came from the forest, and Mary, exclaiming that there
was something wrong, started off in the direction of the
cries. Tom, Mr. Ovens's helper, was sent after her.
Anxiously news was awaited by those around Mr.
Ovens, and when Tom came back saying an accident had
happened and would Mr. Ovens get the restoratives
and come as quickly as possible, fear had overspread
all faces.

Miss Slessor was beside an unconscious young man,
who, she told Mr. Ovens, was Etim, the eldest son of her
chief, Edem. He was engaged in building a house in
preparation for his forthcoming marriage, and in handling
a post (small tree trunk) it had slipped from his grasp,
striking him on the neck. Paralysis had followed.
Wondering at the apprehension in her face, she saw he
did not realise what would happen. Accident is never
accident in these parts, she informed him, but always
witchcraft, violent death the same, and there would be
great trouble.

Between them they bore the young man on an im-

provised litter to Ekenge. There, in his mother's house,
Miss Slessor nursed him, hoping that he would get
better. All in vain, his injuries were too serious ; and
added to that, on the day when he lay dying some natives
came into the chief's enclosure and strove by horrible
means to revive him. Mary heard the noise, and flew
to him, to find ground pepper being rubbed into his
eyes, smoke being blown into his nostrils, his mouth
being forced open, and his uncle bawling into his ears.
It is not surprising that Mary was only in time to have
the dead body presented to her. Edem declared
threateningly that sorcerers had brought the lad to his
untimely end, and they must be killed. Instantly every
one disappeared, with the exception of his weeping
mother. The witch-doctor duly arrived, and a certain
village was named by him as being guilty, and with fearful
hubbub and threats the freemen armed and marched
to the place. All the houses were sacked, those who
could not escape to the forest were put into chains and
taken to the chief's yard at Ekenge.

Mary meanwhile, in the hope of cooling the anger of
Edem and Ekpenyong (father and uncle), arrayed the
poor body in such things as were suitable to honour his
rank. To us the spectacle would be dreadful, but she
did what she knew would please the natives and his
parents. But delight may exceed the bounds of decorum,
and she and Mr. Ovens had to take it turn about to
watch and protect the prisoners all night and day.
Drinking went on, and Mr. Ovens was so disgusted that
he almost refused to make a coffin when " Ma " asked
him to—almost, but not quite. He did make it, and he
stood by her in all the terrible time which followed. She
had a great struggle with chiefs and people to stop the

poison ordeal with eséré beans which was to be administered to the prisoners. The outcome of it all, after a long and intricate contest of wills, was, that Edem gave in, the prisoners by ones and twos were wrested from the avengers, the chief " Akpo " who had run away and so made himself appear guilty (no one was) was brought back, and he and his family allowed to make their homes again in the burnt village. Edem himself forbade any one to take any life for his son's death, and gave the suspected chief ground and seed-plants for food, to plant there. To Mary he (Edem) was very grateful, for she had prevented much bloodshed and horror. He told her they were very weary of the old, terrible ways, but unless all joined to put away the system, he had no power to break it in other tribes.

It was on this occasion that she seized a bag in which there were poison beans. " Only palm nuts and cartridges, Ma." She opened it, and sure enough there were nuts and cartridges, but something made her delve deep, and she unearthed forty beans. She took them, and said she would keep them. Violent protestations. She walked down the line of armed men holding the bag, daring them to take it from her. Their hands seemed powerless to do so, and she walked on, reached her hut, gave the beans to Mr. Ovens, and went back to pour oil on the troubled waters. It was a wonderful triumph for Christ.

When the trouble about the death of Edem's son was over, building was resumed by Mr. Ovens and his assistants. Mary went about her usual daily avocations. Her family now consisted of Janie, Alice, Annie, and Mary, so named after Miss Slessor. Miss Mary Kingsley speaks of this little one in her *Travels in West Africa*.

News of the baby came to Mary through some women
returning from market past her house. She heard them
remark that it was wonderful that it still lived. It had
been thrown out as no one wanted to keep it. Mother
dead, father indifferent. Off went Miss Slessor, and
brought the weeping mite home. Eyes and nose were
swarming with ants, part of the cartilage had been
eaten away, as also had part of the upper lip. Under
Mary's care it soon grew into a pretty, bonnie child.
" One of the prettiest black children I have ever seen,"
wrote Miss Kingsley, and that is saying a great deal,
for negro children are very pretty. She goes on to speak
of their round faces, their immense deer-like eyes, so
melancholy and wondering, their flat little ears, so dainty
in shape. And, we might add, little hearts that have
longings for a Saviour and a Home in Heaven, and of
this " Ma " was teaching them every day. These four were
a comfort to their white " Mother " as the years passed on.

Mr. Ovens fell ill before he had quite made an
end of his work at Ekenge. Miss Slessor nursed him
through a very bad illness, and when he left her village
for Duke Town once more, she missed him greatly. As
for him, he would talk and talk of that time with her.
Her courage in dealing with the natives, drunk or sober,
had amazed him. He had seen her administer a dose of
castor oil to a man who thought it was " witchcraft,"
and she had to administer a good cuff at the same time.
She stopped two tribes from fighting, compelling them
to stack their guns on each side of her. The piles were
about five feet high at the end. She also on another
occasion took possession of a lot of machetes from a
canoe intended for up-river fighting. Fearless indeed
she must have been, for these men could have done what

they willed with her. " If God be for us——" So
Mr. Ovens had plenty to tell.

She had made great progress in securing places where
she could stay. In several villages she had a room built
for her own use, and this gave the people the feeling that
" Ma " was looking after them. She had a boathouse,
built by Mr. Ovens, very useful for housing her canoe
and stores. And in every way she simply lived for
these dark-minded, dark-skinned children of the forest.
Slowly but surely she was getting a hold of them, and
putting down the fearful customs and superstitions which
held them in thrall. One case of twins is very memorable.
The grandmother had murdered the babies, and the
poor mother was stretched out on the cold floor of a hut.
Ma sent her a pillow, and a bed, and had the temerity
to beg her husband to be loving to his suffering, bereaved
wife. He not only treated her kindly, but actually took
her back home !

Often she would be called away miles into the forest,
where the natives had hidden in order to administer the
poison ordeal without her knowledge, and usually she
won the victory and saved lives.

Once Ma Eme's farm was attacked by robbers, and
Miss Slessor spent Sunday there trying to establish peace
among the drinking natives.

Then there was the frequent, " Run, Ma, run ! there
are twins ! " and she would go at once. Up to 1890
she had saved fifty-one twins.

She was also constantly preventing the killing of the
retinue of wives and slaves on the death of a chief.
" Ma," said one man reproachfully, " you have quite
spoilt our fashions. Before you came a man took his
people with him ; now he must go alone."

Then there was the constant attention needed in keeping her home and yard free from the encroachment of the bush. Lovely as these flowering shrubs and trees were, they had to be cut down, for they grew too fast, and offered covering for beasts of prey. She and her girls had to do this, as the natives were so busy now, planting yams for trading with Calabar.

CHAPTER VII

Finding a Mother

IN 1891 she was due to go home on furlough. Arrangements had been made for Miss Dunlop to have charge of the station during Miss Slessor's absence, and packing had begun at Ekenge. The steamer would be up-river to fetch her pretty soon. But there's many a slip—and as " Ma " was ramming things together into boxes, messengers came from a village a long way off to tell her that a young freeman had shot his hand accidentally out hunting. Would " Ma " come and bring medicine? She had to give them directions, instead, for she was too ill and frail for the journey, and expected the steamer any time. If the symptoms became serious they were to let her know. In a very short time she had secret news of the man's death, and that a chief had been injured by his brother. How the news came, or by whom, she never knew, but she started to the village immediately, despite the protestations of all Ekenge, two armed men with her. She also promised to call on another chief eight miles away for a freeman and a drum, so that all in the roused village of the dead man would hear that a protected person was on the way, and must not be harmed.

When at length, after passing bands of warriors who were intent on a fight against the village, she encountered, in the village itself, a solid phalanx of men, and tried to force a way through them, and remarking on their manners for obstructing her. The sullen line remained immovable, when suddenly an old warrior stepped out and greeted her as a friend. It was that same chief for whom she had walked eight hours in the torrential rain soon after her arrival at Okoyong, he who was dying almost, and who had so marvellously recovered under her ministrations. Now she was to reap a reward for the courageous act.

He thanked her for coming. Said they admitted the wounding of the chief, but one man only was to blame, not the whole village. Would she use her influence with their opponents, so that there should be no fighting.

To gain time, and to create a good atmosphere, " Ma " demanded food. And while she satisfied her hunger they were to find a comfortable place in the bush and choose two reliable men of each side, and presently she would come and hear the cause.

The offending parties humbled themselves abjectly, begging that the act of a drunken boy might be forgiven. After some arguing and stormy scenes they finally accepted, and a fine was imposed. Far better than fighting. Mary stayed a long time with them, for some drinking took place. She wished she could have a service, but the atmosphere was too disturbed ; she did, however, quietly talk to them of Christ as Saviour, after which she set out on her dark, lonely walk through the forest. Her baggage had been fetched away, and an escort had arrived to take her to Duke Town.

She arrived in England in January of 1891. Janie was with her, and able to take care of her, as she was now about twelve or thirteen, and had been over with Mary in 1883–84. Mary stayed in the home of Mrs. M'Crindle, Joppa, Midlothian, and from there prosecuted her little-loved deputational work. People were immensely attracted by her, but she was very shy of speaking. It was, however, an ordeal which she had to face, and later the reward appeared in the increased interest as shown by multiplied letters and Mission boxes.

It was during this visit that she dropped a bomb, so to speak, among her admirers. She was engaged to Mr. Charles W. Morrison on the Duke Town Mission staff. He was a man of great literary talent, and had always admired Mary, and when she was ill at Duke Town, had been very good to her. Before she went to England on furlough, January 1891, they had become engaged, and hoped they would work together at Okoyong. When the Foreign Mission Board were consulted about it, they were some time coming to a decision. Mr. Morrison asked Mary if she would come back to Duke Town if the Board refused consent to his going to Okoyong. She gave an unqualified refusal. To leave Okoyong without a worker for a place where teachers and Bibles abounded was unthinkable, she said. Should God not send Mr. Morrison to Okoyong he must work where he was placed, and so must she. It looks as if the Board had doubts of the wisdom of the arrangement, and eventually they spoke of the good he was doing in Duke Town. Things must remain so for the present. Mary took it as the right answer, and as from the Lord. Not long afterwards Mr. Morrison had to go home on account of ill health, and being advised by a specialist not to return to Calabar, he suggested he might be appointed to Kaffraria. There was no opening there, and consequently he resigned. Later he went to America, North Carolina, living in the balsam woods in a hut. The place and all his literary labours were burnt up, and his feeble health could not stand the shock. He died very shortly afterwards.

Whilst Mary was in England she had a bad attack of influenza, and was sent down to Devonshire for a time; but she was anxious to finish all her deputation work, and having addressed many meetings, and written a letter to *The Record* about training the natives in industrial handicrafts and trades, which caused a big stir, for the Calabar Committee were very favourable to it, she gladly packed up and with Janie sailed once more for Africa. The Topsham visit, where she had spent the beginning and the end of her furlough, and looked upon the graves of her mother and sister, faded into a dream-like vision, and work at Okoyong filled her horizon once more.

Ma Eme would be glad to see her again, and resumed her post of secret intelligence officer, keeping Mary informed of any horrors about to be perpetrated, thus enabling her to prevent a great number of crimes. The secret sign between the women was very simple. When anything was afoot, and Mary was to be ready to dash off at a moment's notice, Ma Eme would send to her for medicine which was to be put in a certain bottle, brought to Mary by Ma Eme's unconscious messenger. The sight of that bottle would set Mary Slessor's senses on the alert. On one occasion, after its appearance, she did not undress at night for weeks, in order to be ready. At last she did, and that night was the night she was compelled to rush out, and with no time but to don the scantiest attire. More than once, when she heard of a palaver to be held which would end in bloodshed, she delayed it by dispatching a sealed sheet of paper, containing just any words, to the chiefs. Whilst they examined and discussed the strange important-looking document, she had time to join them, and with her knitting, sitting beside the chief, guide things to a more peaceful issue than they would have done without her.

When she could she slipped down to Duke Town to enjoy the society of the ladies of the Mission there, and attending the meetings. Her family went with her and found accommodation easily, until she considered them too numerous. Then she would walk half-way to Adiabo, on the Calabar River, where the Mission friends met her, and all, with the food each had brought, had a merry picnic.

But she longed for a helper at Okoyong. The work was a scramble, she said, and she felt sad because she was not doing it as it should be done. But she taught her little scholars a love of flowers which they had never noticed though always surrounded by them. They made the home very pretty, and she had made a private path to the spring so that her girls need not come into contact with the women. This path, shaded with flowering trees and starry jasmine, had to be kept under control, so fast did things grow. And all around, lovely shrubs and coarser things had to be hacked back as they encroached upon the walls and dwellings. Mary and her girls did this, for the villagers were busy planting and tending crops for trade with Calabar to help her often.

There is a story Mary often told, so deeply did it touch her. Edem had bought a beautiful young girl for one of his chief men, and Ma Eme, had brought one of her own slave-women from the farm to the village, a move not at all pleasing to the woman, as she preferred the farm to the village. The new slave Edem had bought heard the woman grumbling, and something in the voice roused memories in the girl's mind. She ran out and looked at the owner of the voice—crept nearer, gazing at the face. "What are you looking at?" the woman asked, surprised. On this, the girl flung her arms round the woman's neck, saying a word in a strange tongue. It was the woman's name, not as others knew it, and after gazing earnestly at the young girl she recognised her own daughter! The mother had been stolen many years before on the occasion of one of those periodical raids on villages. A little while after Mary, visiting Ma Eme, found her with the reunited pair, sitting beside a log fire, and the girl told them how she had prayed to the great God that she, too, might be captured, and have the opportunity of looking for her mother in Duke Town, and here—in Ekenge—she found her!

And so life went on at Ekenge. Mary's house became more and more a Children's Hospital. Parents would bring frail ones to be nursed back to health and strength, and then fetched home again. Children put aside by unloving relatives who would not be bothered. Outcast babies—twins, the horror of all! Mary made all welcome, and many an agonised baby passed from her loving care up to Him who said, " Suffer the little children to come unto Me." Poor little broken bodies, soothed as far as " Ma " could do it, often she was glad when the last fluttering breath was drawn, and the spirit took its flight beyond all pain, to realms of light and love, never more to suffer.

And the poor mothers of twins were always treated so brutally. There was a slave-woman owned by a kind mistress, but when she bore twins nothing was bad enough for her. All her English possessions were smashed up, she was thrust out of her village with the babies (pushed down into a calabash) on her head, together with various cooking utensils, and would have been killed but for fear of " Ma." " Ma " had heard all about her plight, and was on the way to meet her in the forest and bring her home. This meant cutting a fresh path up to the Mission House, for the natives never would have used that Mission House path again had Miss Slessor brought the twins that way. Miss Mary Kingsley had just arrived on a visit to Miss Slessor, and witnessed the scene when the twins and their outcast mother arrived with Miss Slessor. One of the babies was dead—the boy—and was buried. The girl was alive, and responded to Miss Slessor's care. The mother, as soon as she was better, returned to her mistress. The mistress was sufficiently enlightened to have her again, provided she did not bring the child. Susie, they called the little thing. She learnt to call Miss Slessor, " Mem, mem." Mary loved her intensely, and when she died, as the result of an accident (pulling a jug of hot water over herself placed near her by a native girl), Mary was heart-broken. Whilst the baby (only fourteen months old) lingered at death's door, all the people, chiefs, and head-men refused to go to market, staying instead to comfort " Ma." Miss Murray, who was helping Mary at that time, buried her, as Mary was too broken to do so. And all the people witnessed that touching little service, reverently and sadly, standing round the grave of a twin ! A prominent woman—a pronounced heathen—actually thanked the God of the white woman for the little girl, praying for a like hope beyond death, which shows what an impression was made by the service.

The slave-mother had often visited the child, and

had learnt to love her. Now she was grief-stricken. Eventually Miss Slessor bought the woman, and set her free, training her to be useful about the Mission House, in view of her being of use to any lady who took Miss Slessor's absence on furlough. Her name was Iye.

CHAPTER VIII

Losing Friends

A BEAUTIFUL day. The "smoking canoe," *David Williamson*, chugging up the Calabar River. This little steamer had been given by children of the Sunday schools in Scotland, and was a source of ceaseless wonder and admiration to the natives; moreover, there were such beautiful things on board, and more white people came to see "Ma."

No matter whether the announcement of its coming was made in the day or at night, every one roused up. Fires were poked up, kettles filled, rooms set in readiness for guests, parcels taken from new white people with breathless interest were laid by with care. To Miss Slessor were given letters—also to wait a bit, while she made her visitors comfortable. After that, many journeys to the beach. Heavy trunks were opened there, packages were made of a size for a person to carry on head, and a long file of jubilant porters bore the loads in single file up to the Mission House, returning many times for more.

At the Mission House followed a grand show. Dressing-gowns—one of which became the Court gown of a chief —baby garments, dainty and sweet. Fancy a mere baby wearing such beautiful things. Among her personal gifts Mary always looked for sweets, and there, sure enough, she would find them after a time hidden away in order to make her search protracted!

She used to write to the children who had given the
" smoking canoe " a very graphic account of its arrival,
and the excitement and joy it brought to her people, as
well as to herself. Those letters must have been pro-
ductive of a deepened interest in Missions. I think many
might be able to date the wish to go as a missionary from
the reception of those vivid word-pictures, as enchanted
boys and girls listened to them.

And now to a less peaceful scene. Miss Slessor heard
of a palaver going on, but a tornado prevented her going.
She managed to get a message to the chief, asking him to
do nothing until she was able to be present. It was a
case of witchcraft. A man was supposed to have caused
his master's death, and he was to suffer the poison ordeal.
When the chief received her request, he ordered the man
to be taken away out of her reach. He meant to follow
out the usual custom in spite of her. She made up her
mind this time to ask the Government to save the man,
and also to bring the horrible custom to an end. The
fact that she had made this appeal scared the offending
parties badly. The man had already escaped to Mary's
place, but all his relatives had been taken and chained
instead. Then, reflecting on the power of the Consul, the
chief set them all free, and went to plead with " Ma."
Would she use her influence with the Consul, so that it
should not be war but peace ? Taking the escaped man
with her she went to Duke Town, and the Consul agreed
to come to her village, where the chiefs were to meet him
for a conference. She allayed the fear of the chiefs, and
warned them of the subjects for discussion.

Then one day Mr. Moore, vice-consul, arrived with a
small guard of honour. The brilliant little cortège marched
imposingly into the enclosure, thrilling the spectators to

the bone. Miss Slessor was fetched from the roof of her house, where she was engaged in repairing leaky portions, and the conference began. Mr. Moore spoke very kindly and with great patience to the chiefs, pointing out that their customs were very evil, and they must make a change for the better. Listening to him with the utmost respect and attention they promised that there should not be any more killing for funerals, and that twins should not be slain, " Ma " to be given the chance of caring for them in a hut specially built for the purpose. This was a great deal to promise. Miss Slessor was very thankful. Nevertheless, she did not dare cease her vigilant watch. But her confidence was yet to bud. A month after this memorable conference an old and wealthy chief died suddenly. Now what ? Mary asked herself. But she refrained from visiting in order to mount guard, only sending presents and compliments, and a reminder of the promise. And no one was missing We may safely say that this was the first time that such a thing had happened in Okoyong. What the witch-doctors thought, history does not relate.

And so, step by step, progress is made. To many it does not look like progress, but those who understand the native mind can see it. Mary saw this sort of " Is-it-any-better " feeling in the mind of Mrs. Weir, who spent a week-end at Ekenge. It was rather fortunate that they visited a village where a chief had died, where Mary used frequently to hold services, and in his grave saw all small personal possessions—snuff-box, powder-flask, and so on, ready for the other world. Mrs. Weir, Mary could see, was surprised and disappointed at the superstition remaining, after the years of labour bestowed on the district. Easily, keen-witted Mary read the thought.

She pointed to the villagers standing about, sad, but not in fear. " All these would be waiting in chains to die, or hiding in the forests, not walking free like this, but for what they have learnt," she said quietly. Surely something had been achieved.

In 1895 there was more twin-killing, and she got Sir Claude Macdonald to come up and repeat what had been said before. He gently but firmly informed them that they must be obedient to the good things the white men asked them to promise. The white man had not come to take their country, but to show them how to govern it wisely, so that every one might be happy, safe, and at peace. Therefore the dreadful old customs must be put away. They had made a promise to do this.

An aged native asked permission for all to adjourn in order to talk together. After a brief conferring he returned and informed Sir Claude that since the white man's words had been repeated they should be obeyed, for unless there was repetition his people never considered there was value in the words. His people would do what the Government wished. The terrible subject of twins was settled thus : " Ma " should have immediate notification of births, as she had promised to look after the children ; but they could on no account take them into their own homes, and Mary felt grateful for this advance. It was balm to her tried spirit. A reward for steadfastness and courage. She sowed her seed in the morning, and in the evening she withheld not her hand, not knowing which should prosper, whether this or that, and she got surprises now and again, and proved " blessed are ye that sow beside all waters."

In a happy way she puts it : " Christ sent me to preach the Gospel, and He will look after results."

She never put in numbers those who professed Christianity, but she knew that when the time came there would be many who could be admitted to the Lord's Supper. She could also say that the chiefs and people who submitted to the rule of the white man's rule found more liberty, not less. Human life was far safer. The inhuman raids, looting, slave-stealing were growing less and less.

In 1896 the people having moved on to better agricultural areas, Miss Slessor had to follow. The new station was at Akpap, more inland and nearer the Cross River, though six miles away from that, and seemed rather inaccessible at first. However, the " smoking canoe " plied frequently up and down. The Calabar Committee gave permission for the move. The landing-place was called Ikenutu, and the track which led to Akpap was the usual old kind of bush path—palms, orange trees, bananas, ferns—and flowers bordered and overhung it in summer, but in the rainy season thick grass, higher than a man, obliterated it, and it was impassable to a stranger without a guide. A good Mission House was to be erected at Akpap, and at Ikenutu beach a shed for storing goods from the " smoking canoe."

Miss Slessor did not wait for the house at Akpap, but installed herself there in a small shed, divided into two rooms. There she and the " family " of little waifs resided. Shortly after this move small-pox broke out. It was all over the country, and in her district she vaccinated people for hours every day. At Ekenge it was very bad indeed. She turned her old house there into a hospital, and many came to it. Others fled from the place, and she could not get any help in burying or nursing.

To her great grief, Ekpenyong died, and, harder than all, Edem, her true friend and chief, passed away when attacked by the disease, after she had made a gallant fight for his life. It was midnight when he died, and in the darkness of the forest she dug his grave, made a coffin, placed him inside, and sorrowfully covered the poor mortal remains. That was the last of the staunch friend.

Weary, lonely, she tramped to Akpap, and just as day was breaking fell asleep. Mr. Ovens and Mr. Alexander awakened her. Mr. Ovens had come to build the house; Mr. Alexander, captain of the " smoking canoe," had brought him up-river. It was helpful to have the company of Mr. Ovens, and building began. Mr. Alexander went to the old house at Ekenge; it was full of dead, and would never be habitable again. The bush soon engulfed it.

Christmas brought some cheer. The Consul-General and Colonel Boisragon of the consular staff were there three days helping to enliven things. There were sweets, biscuits, fruit, and all manner of nice eatables, toys and dolls. These must have been procured from some steamer by the Government officials.

In 1898 she was sent to Scotland. Before she left Duke Town a box from Renfield Street Church, Glasgow, arrived, and in it she found all she and the children needed for the voyage. A shawl was one of the treasures, and the poor, weary frame felt comfortable and protected by it. She had to be carried on board, but on the voyage experienced God's loving care all the time. She knew He would not fail her in her time of weakness and need. And her faith in her friend Mrs. M'Crindle, Joppa, was fully justified. Just a telegram on arrival at Liverpool, and there was the trustworthy hostess at Waverley Station, Edinburgh, ready on this short notice to receive Miss Slessor, to say nothing of Janie, Alice, Mary, and Maggie, the last-named only sixteen months.

After this came the usual deputational work which awakened great interest. She pleaded for people, not money. She reminded them that thousands had answered Kitchener's call for men for the Soudan, and she asked her audience where were the soldiers of the cross? Hundreds of officers and men had gone to offer themselves in a recent African war. There was a Royal prince among them. But, alas! the Banner of the Cross—the ensign of the King of kings—that stands alone.

Christmas was spent on the steamer. She had many invitations at places they entered, but she did not accept any, needing all the rest and quiet she could get; at the same time the loving thought cheered her much.

So work in Okoyong began again. In December 1899 Janie or Jean, as she was called, was married. Akibo Eyo was her husband's name, one of Mary's best scholars. They went to Ma Eme's farm. But something happened; it is not quite clear what that was, but Jean came to Miss Slessor once more, and there remained till the end.

Okoyong was settling down into a peaceful territory under " Ma's " influence. Even more than one native had been known to take back his wife after she had given birth to twins, and a twin boy had been kept by his parents. Drinking was on the decrease, palavers were not so often scenes of bloodshed and quarrels.

One Government official says of her, that as an interpreter she made every palaver an easy one to settle, because she could represent to each side exactly what the other party wished to say.

She was even called upon to settle a dispute between the Umon and Okoyong, the Umon people being confident that she would mete out justice even if it went against her own side.

As she was going up-river to this palaver, there was an adventure with a hippopotamus which attacked the canoe, but happily no harm was done.

Later on, much against her will, she was ordered back to Creek Town, as the Government were obliged to send out troops against the Aros, who refused to submit to Government authority. During this unwilling absence Okoyong remained quiet and true, and she returned rather earlier than the Government had intended her to !

On the fifteenth anniversary of her arrival at Ekenge, the twenty-ninth year of her missionary career, a happy company gathered round the first memorial table in Okoyong.

How different this from the first sad Sunday. Looking back over the fifteen years, Mary could see how tenderly she had been led, and how wonderfully God had blessed her work ; and when the 103rd Psalm (old metrical version in native tongue) was raised, her heart was raised too in adoration and love.

CHAPTER IX

Love so Amazing

ONCE more the pioneering spirit is urging Miss Slessor forward. Akpap could now be left to others, and she herself could go where for many years she had yearned to go—Enyong Creek.

She therefore starts negotiations for two ladies to come to Akpap, and, pending settlement, she, in her usual prompt manner, canoed up to Itu with two of her boys, Esien and Effiom, and Mana one of her girls, settling them there to teach school and take services, an experiment which proved successful far beyond " Ma's " hopes— abundantly above all she asked or thought. This was in 1903.

At Arochuku, after Miss Wright was settled in Akpap, she did the same thing, and when she was embarking for home she was pressed on all hands to come back soon.

She lay back in her canoe, thanking God for prospering her undertakings, and admiring the loveliness of the landscape around her. Enyong Creek, the scene of most fearful wickedness and anguish, the hotbed of slave-trade and superstition, was beautiful. Tropical trees lined the banks, their branches often interlacing—the fallen trunks having their hollows full of lovely orchids and ferns ; the surface of the water bearing pretty water lilies ; blue kingfishers and yellow palm birds flitting through the foliage overhead as the canoe slips softly along the water-way.

But amidst all this loveliness there is the fearful sore of sin and sorrow, the crying need for messengers to bring the needs of the Saviour of mankind to the dark and sin-stained inhabitants.

Miss Slessor knew all about the Aros and the Long Juju, with its wily slave-trade system. Whilst in Okoyong she had had visitors from Arochuku, with their tales of cruelty and wrong, and had already won a place in the hearts of many of their chiefs. And now she had received a welcome from the men who themselves were responsible for the wicked slave traffic carried on by the superstition of the Long Juju, and had stood on the very spot itself where the iniquitous practice was carried on.

Small wonder that her heart was lifted up in praise that morning as she progressed quietly homewards in her canoe. God was about to do great things.

But suddenly another canoe shot out across the river and collided, quite politely, with hers.

The man in it had a wonderful story to tell, and a letter for her, which resulted in " Ma " there and then going to see the writer of the letter at Akani Obio. His name was Onoyom Iya Nya, and he had been chosen by the Government as President of the Native Court. Also he was the only chief in the district who had not been dis-armed by the Government.

Well, this man, Onoyom, met Mary when his servant brought her to his beach, and told her he was seeking God ; had been seeking Him a long while. There is not space to tell all the story. It went back to his boyhood in 1875, when a white man had appeared in the Creek, sending the natives flying in fear, except this boy.

The white man had come to tell the story of Jesus. He was Dr. Robb, from Ikorofiong. At one time Mammy

Fuller had been nurse in his family. Dr. Robb persuaded the boy to lead him to the chiefs, and when he was with them, preached to them words which the boy, at least, never forgot.

But he grew up a heathen, and had suffered great sorrow. Now he wanted " Ma " to lead him to Jesus. The Lord Jesus Himself has promised (and He keeps His promises) that they who seek Him shall find Him. Onoyom found Him at last, and became one of His truest followers.

He had the courage to hew down a grand tree, around which was gathered much juju superstition, and turned it into seats for the church he built. Better still, he put away all his wives, save one, making ample provision for them. The wife he kept was a twin-mother whom he had once turned away. His town was a prohibition town, and on Sundays a white flag was raised to show that there was no Sunday trading. He also built a bridge over the Creek.

In 1904 she was due for furlough, but spent the time viewing Enyong Creek for sites for Mission Stations and rest-houses. Chief Onoyom was visited, not only by Miss Slessor and Miss Wright, but by Mr. and Mrs. Wilkie. Mr. Wilkie had come out to see the place where Miss Slessor wanted a Medical Station up the Creek. They were all charmed by Chief Onoyom. At one village an old chief showed them a lot of books—Bibles and *Pilgrim's Progress* among them. He had had a son who was anxious to learn book and " God Palavers," so had purchased the books and found some one to teach the lad. But, alas ! the son had died two months before, and the father was heart-broken. He begged Mary not to leave him until he had " found God." He did find Him very shortly, and as a Christian his happiness was sweet and lasting.

There were the beginnings of Mission Stations at several places along the Creek—Okpo, Akani (Onoyom's place), Obio, Odot, and Asang. The young teachers she established in various villages worked splendidly teaching school and telling the old, old story, now so precious to themselves. Etim, one of the boys, was at Ikotobong; he was to be given food by the people, and Miss Slessor paid him five shillings a week out of her own pocket. All this itinerating was not to be any expense to the Foreign Mission Board. They were to take measures later. Jean was at Okpo, teaching the girls and women. Some of the tiny stations contributed several pounds each to the new churches which were building at Akani and Asang.

Eight members of Presbytery were present at the opening of Akani Obio. Then they went to Asang. So Miss Slessor was having her wish more than fulfilled. She had more than once thought of " earning her own chop " and enough for her bairns, and going forward on her pioneering on her own account, for to her the Home Base seemed rather slow in moving at times. The Mission Board recognised at length her abilities as a pioneer, and she was set free to press forward. Her assurance that the small native-taught stations would be practically self-supporting was justified again and again.

The girls who were constantly with her attended to her needs with truest affection. At dawn, if " Ma " awakened, a Bible and a cup of steaming hot tea were there. She was cheered by the confession of Alice, a beautiful girl who had been with her from babyhood; Alice crept up to her side one night to say that she had accepted the Saviour.

The Government, seeing her influence with the natives, invested her with the power of magistrate. She undertook the work, but refused remuneration. Her popularity in court was great, for the natives got their causes heard first hand owing to her perfect knowledge of their tongue, and the Government officials had implicit confidence in her judgment on account of her clear insight and intimate knowledge of native life and character.

It was not an unusual thing for " Ma " to box the ears of a truculent witness or abusive chief in court, and she was held in fear and awe by the natives everywhere. The Government officials esteemed her highly, many of them reverencing her as a mother.

In 1907 she was so ill that she was ordered home to Scotland, and Government officials vied with each other in making her journey easy, as also did her fellow-workers. Mr. Gray packed for her, Mr. Middleton of Lagos undertook to care for her on the voyage, and she reached Edinburgh at last with a heart full of gratitude to them.

She and Dan, the little six-years-old boy whom she had brought with her, stayed with her dear friend, Mrs. M'Crindle. Miss Slessor was soon nearly overwhelmed by her correspondence. Parcels, post cards, letters, and invitations were showered upon her. She paid visits to several friends, and went out cycling with some of them. But the civilised roads in Britain were not so pleasant to her as bush paths in Africa. So timid was she that if she saw a dog coming along she got off her machine at once, nor would she remount until the dog had passed.

She addressed several meetings. People expected she would address a great many, but she announced her intention of returning to Calabar in October, though only a few months of her furlough were spent. She was not happy. She had heard by letter a story about one of her beloved girls in Africa, and was anxious to get back and see what it meant. As far as we know she said nothing about it, and bravely carried out her engagements, having her reward in large and reverent gatherings, to whom she gave vivid pictures of the life and work in Calabar and the need for more workers. She did not write or prepare speeches beforehand, but spoke simply out of her over-flowing heart. On the last night of her stay, her friends found her weeping bitterly and realising her solitariness very keenly, for there were none of her own kith and kin. She felt also that life over here was too hurried, and filled with too many things. Very possibly she thought some of them a waste of time, and perhaps she was right. " Ma's " heart was in Africa. She was glad to find herself once more on the way there, and seemed to gain a new lease of life during the voyage.

On her arrival, her loving, anxious heart was rejoiced to find that the unhappy story (which had been circulated by a native) was entirely without foundation.

And so ended Miss Slessor's last furlough in Britain. Would it have troubled her had she known it was her last ? I think not. She had no home ties here, but in Africa she had vast—one may say eternal—interests, where she was doing a work for eternity. There was the scheme of a Home for Women and Girls to be carried out, there were new stations to be planted, natives in an area of over two thousand miles looked to her for advice and help. Even in Northern Nigeria they knew the brave white " Ma."

Use was her headquarters, and as soon as she felt free to move in the matter she purchased a site for the Home in the name of her girls (being European, she could not purchase in her own), with the consent and help of the Government.

Then, as there was a period of waiting, she quietly went on planting the fruit trees sent by the Government. She also began to accumulate stock, her first memorable instalment being a cow, which she bought from a man to prevent his going to prison for debt. This cow was a terror to the natives, and was always getting loose. It ran away even when "Ma" and the Principal of the Hope-Waddell Institute were leading it gently home one day. It was more famous than "the cow with the crumpled horn."

But all this time Miss Slessor was growing weaker and more broken down in health; the frail body was not equal to the strong, brave spirit, and she was several times laid aside.

She felt that she ought to give up her court work, as she had so much to do in spreading the Gospel, and sent in her resignation, which was regretfully accepted.

One of her girls, Mary, was married to the young native driver of the Government motor-car at this time, and shortly afterwards followed the first baptismal and communion services at Use—Use, only a short time since dark, degraded, and drink-sodden.

But "Ma" felt now that there was also work for her farther afield than Use. Some young men from Ikpe had come to her, and she had influenced them so strongly that they wished to become "God men," and had gone back to Ikpe to begin a Christian work there. Now they had come to "Ma" again and told her there were forty others ready to become Christians.

Ikpe was two days away from Use by water, an old slave centre in a degraded part of Northern Nigeria, and in league with Aro. Services were held on Sunday and weekdays, and these young teachers knew only the most elementary truths as yet. What could " Ma " do in face of such heart-hunger as was manifested by these poor groping natives ?

She went to them several times, but at last their reproaches that she did no more touched her so deeply that she said, " *I am coming.*"

In a short time she did return, with corrugated iron and other material for her building, and so the work began.

She still had Use as headquarters, making the journey to and fro by canoe. But it was too much for her, and in 1911, when repairing her tornado-ruined home at Use, she collapsed. At the time, Dr. Robertson's place at Itu was temporarily filled by Dr. Hitchcock, a young man, quite as masterful in his way as was " Ma," and she eventually found she had to submit to his orders. He even had the temerity to send her fowls, as she was not feeding herself suitably for her state of health. On one occasion, she asked him why he had sent that fowl ; to which inquiry he promptly replied that he was obliged to, as it could not come by itself, and that was all the answer " Ma " got.

It was a long time before she was at Ikpe again, and even then it was only by running away from the doctor. A great throng received her on the beach, and she was overjoyed to be at work once more. She established Jean at Nkanga as teacher and evangelist, where she had one shilling a week, and food from the people, and " Ma " provided her clothes. Jean was the best Efik teacher Mary knew, and her knowledge of the Scriptures very thorough.

Miss Slessor always looked upon money—even that given for her personal needs—as a help only for forwarding the work of God. A Government cheque for £25 for herself, in recognition of her work, was destined for her Home for Women ; and so on with all that came. Thus it sometimes happened, in spite of abundant funds in Duke Town in her name, that in Ikpe and like places she was often hard put to it to find the wherewithal to purchase food.

The boxes of clothing, etc., which were sent out by the Church were a cause of much pleasurable excitement. In 1911 shortbread and buns were enclosed, and this was doubly happy, for bush food had been upsetting her, and a diet of shortbread and buns for a week made her better.

The people around were kind, too, and saw to it that yams and rice were forthcoming from time to time, ostensibly, " for the children."

But " Ma " was steadily growing weaker, and the gift of a Cape cart in which she could be pushed along by two boys or girls was a great joy. In bygone days she had twice had a gift of a bicycle, but her cycling days were past.

In this Cape cart, or basket-chair on wheels, " Ma " was able to do more work in the way of looking for building sites for churches. It was her wish to make a series of churches and schools in Ibibio.

This scheme, and the basket-chair, put a stop to her idea of going home on furlough, and in September 1912 she completed her thirty-sixth year as a missionary by making tours along the Government road, opening up out-stations wherever she could gather the natives in their villages.

CHAPTER X

The Last Years

AND now " Ma " was to have what she considered her first real holiday, though it appears she was almost ashamed to have such a glorious time.

Her health had given concern in Scotland and in Calabar, and a lady on the Foreign Mission Board at home succeeded in persuading Miss Slessor to go to an hotel in Grand Canary, since the cold of an English or Scots winter would be too severe for her. Friends prepared her outfit—making her, as she quaintly said, " wise-like and decent "—and Janie went with her. Mr. Wilkie handed the cash-box to the captain, he in turn passed it on to the other captain when she transhipped, and he, again, on arrival at Grand Canary gave it to the manager of Hotel Santa Catalina, where she put up, and during the whole of her stay the management treated her with the utmost deference and love.

The change did her good, the days spent in the sunny grounds and on the hillsides were days she never forgot, and she returned to Use to find that she was frustrated in her intention of paying for it herself, for Miss Cook, the Foreign Mission Board friend, had settled the entire cost.

Shortly after this holiday, much to her chagrin, one of her eyes was injured by a pellet of mud. Erysipelas followed, she was blind and in much pain and fever for a fortnight, but as soon as possible, she was at Ikpe again, though the eye was still troublesome.

The building at Ikpe progressed, and " Ma " was very busy with all the work on her hands. Her heart ached for those who were yet unreached, and she longed for more missionaries to be sent out.

But even in all this bustle she yearned for letters and news. She once said she was seven weeks without a word from the outside. All the reading matter she had was old advertisement sheets which lined her boxes. From these she declared she had learnt the names of all hotels and boarding-houses in any part of Europe, and was willing to give the information to any one who asked for it.

When any stray white visitor appeared with papers and letters it was a glorious day. Let us remember, if we cannot *be* missionaries, we can *cheer* missionaries, if we will, by writing and sending papers.

Government officials always visited her when in her neighbourhood, and the relations between them were friendly and happy. To some of them her introductions were decidedly informal in character. A stranger appeared one day when she was busy on the roof of the house. Looking down upon him critically, she asked what he wanted, and he, hat in hand, replied meekly that he was her new District Commissioner, but he couldn't help it. She was charmed, and at once adopted him as a friend.

A great official, whose wife was writing to Mary, added as postscript to his wife's letter : " *She* sends her kindest regards ; *I* send my love."

The Government gave instructions that she was to be allowed to make use of any conveyance belonging to them, and that all possible help was to be given to her.

And from these same officials she received books,

magazines, papers, etc., and sweets, crackers, and plum pudding at Christmas. On one Christmas Day several of them came and spent the day with her. The Governor of Southern Nigeria, Lord Egerton, with three or four officials, paid her a visit one dark, showery night, and left a case of milk, two cakes, and boxes of chocolate and crystallised fruit. He and she were delighted with each other. In the eagerness of conversing she said once to him : " Hoots, my dear laddie—I mean, sir."

" Ma " valued letters from her friends, and still more did she value their prayers. And in later years when she prayed for them her petition was : " Lord, give them Thy best, and it shall suffice them and me." How wise, how trustful !

Her Heavenly Father was so near, so real to her, that she talked to Him as to a friend walking beside her, and her Bibles were full of marginal notes and remarks which showed how unspeakably precious the Book was to her.

In 1913 she revisited Akpap, and there was, of course, one great unending reception during the whole of her stay. Ma Eme was with her an entire day, and their reminiscences of bygone days were intensely interesting to both. Ma Eme was still a heathen, alas ! and shortly after this visit she died. It was a great grief to Mary that she, this dear, brave, stately black woman, never came out on the side of Christ.

There was a service arranged during Mary's visit, and it had to be held in the unfinished church, for there were more than four hundred well-dressed natives present to hear " Ma."

One day, soon after her stay at Akpap, came a most august-looking document for her. It asked her to accept

the honour of Honorary Associate of the Order of the
Hospital of St. John of Jerusalem in England. " Ma "
was astonished, and eventually accepted.

Soon came another letter signifying the approval of
King George and his sanction to her election. " Ma "
said nothing about it, hoping to keep the matter secret,
but the badge, a silver Maltese Cross, came through the
Colonial Office to the Commissioners at Duke Town,
and so she had to submit to a formal presentation there,
and a Government launch was sent to fetch her.

The villages round Ikpe were not as responsive to
" Ma " as others had been, but by degrees she made
headway.

On the Government road at Odoro Ikpe was a Government Rest House. She climbed up to it one Saturday.
It had a doorway, but no door ; only holes for windows,
and a mud floor, but to her it represented a fortress
from which to attack the surrounding villages, and she
appropriated it, knowing well that the Government would
not object.

Of course, as always, there was the fight over twins and
twin-mothers. The chiefs were firm and " Ma " was
firm. At Ibam, when she asked to start a mission there
she was advised to go home and let them think it over !

Odoro Ikpe was her next venture, and she gained a
solid foothold there after a long palaver. This advance
was regarded somewhat sorrowfully by the Ikpe Christians,
and they asked if she was forsaking them. She could
not do that, so, at this time she was keeping three centres
going—Use, Ikpe, and Odoro Ikpe.

But more yet.

One Sunday morning during service she noticed six
strange men enter. After service they told her they were

from Ibam (the place where she had been told to go
home and let them think it over), and asked her to come
to them, and they would build a place to worship God.
They gave their *best* yard, and crowds attended the meetings.   Ibam was the last heathen stronghold in that
district, and, it having surrendered, Miss Slessor wrote
to her friends in the homeland saying that she was the
most grateful and most joyful woman alive.   What did
it matter that she only had the floor of the Rest House
to sit on, her tired back against a mud wall, her only
light a candle held upright by its own grease?   The rest
of the weary, the Light of the World, was being preached
all around, and God was blessing her work.

One incident at Ikpe I must not miss.   " Ma " was
holding a service at Ikpe, and to her amazement thirty
lads from Odoro Ikpe came in.   So interested and so
earnest were they now, that they had walked five miles to
hear " Ma " speak of the Lord Jesus Christ.   The Ikpe
people, on the entrance of the strangers, got up at once
and gave them their seats, taking up a position on the
floor themselves.   What a lesson in Christian politeness !

The discovery of coal in Udi, and the starting of a
railway from Port Harcourt to that place, brought before
Miss Slessor's far-seeing mind the vital need of more
workers among the numbers of heathen who would
congregate in the new centres of industry.

Very frequent were her calls to those across the sea,
telling them of this great need, and much was she grieved
by the apathy of Christians in Britain.

> " *Can* we, whose souls are lighted
>   With wisdom from on high—
> *Can* we to men benighted,
>   The lamp of life deny ? "

But Mary Slessor was not apathetic. She pursued her way. Wherever she could she built her little wattle and daub churches, and in them preached the simple Gospel to the natives. She was greatly averse to elaborate churches. She feared to put anything forward save Christ. The simplest form of worship in an environment of their own setting made for purer, clearer understanding of Divine things, she believed, and surely she was right. She never spent the money given on expensive or ornate buildings, but in pioneer work among the tribes.

The house at Odoro Ikpe was a long time in course of erection ; the men and boys employed were the laziest and greediest she had ever tackled, and during her occasional absences at Use the work was always badly done.

But it was finished at last, somewhat in the rough, and by means of a ladder " Ma " climbed up to the top rooms to sit on the loosely boarded floor whilst tending her latest motherless baby, gazing meantime across the wild African plain.

Brave woman, *lonely* woman humanly speaking, but she knew that He who will never leave us nor forsake us was there. Her spirit was dauntless, though her body was weak and broken.

This was July 1914. Then came whispers along the African bush paths of strange things happening in the great world across the sea.

Why had canoes laden with produce returned unloaded ? Why had trading come to a sudden end ? Why did not the building materials come ?

Louder and louder grew the whispers, until in wild panic natives came and told her of awful tragedies in Europe. Britain and France at war with Germany !

She could not believe it, and bravely continued her station duties in order to calm her people. But she sent for food in case it were true, and found prices already doubled and her difficulties thereby increased.

Then came the real blow—her first war mail. Hitherto the Government official at Ikot Ekpene had given her some news, but not the worst. Now she had the unvarnished account of the brutal invasion of Belgium and the reverses of the Allied Armies.

The shock struck her down. As a matter of fact, she does not seem ever to have really recovered from this. The thought of dying alone in the bush at the Government Rest House troubled her, on account of a fear that her skull might be seized and worshipped as a powerful juju by the people. After a fortnight of intermittent, raging fever, she was conveyed by her boys and girls to Okopedi beach. There a trading agent sent at once for Dr. Wood at Itu, and she was taken to Use, when, realising how near the end she might be, she asked Miss Peacock to come over to her. Miss Peacock knew that " Ma " must be very ill before she would send for help, and she set off on her bicycle for Use at once.

There was a small measure of improvement later, but Miss Peacock and Miss Couper, who both visited her, now noticed that her old rallying power was gone. She consented gladly to an offer made by her dear friend, Mrs. Arnot, now a widow, of a home with her during this visit to the old country. The idea was that she should finish the house at Odoro Ikpe and leave in spring for Scotland.

But the Lord whom they both served had other plans for these two dear women. Mrs. Arnot was to be missionary in charge of the memorial to her friend—

" The Mary Slessor Home for Women and Girls "—and Mary would be at Home with the Lord, for after a few days' illness her call to higher service came on the morning of January 13, 1915, in the sixty-sixth year of her age and the thirty-ninth of her missionary life.

She was buried at Duke Town. Missionaries, Government officials, merchants, were there. Flags were flying at half-mast. The coffin was draped with the Union Jack, and borne shoulder-high by the boat boys. Crowds watched the silent procession to the grave on Mission Hill. There a wail began as the coffin approached, but Mammy Fuller, sitting alone at the top of the grave, rose, saying : " Do not cry—do not cry ! Praise God from whom all blessings flow. ' Ma ' was a great blessing."

And so, amid a silent, weeping throng, the short, simple service was conducted by Mr. Wilkie, and, when the last sounds of " Asleep in Jesus " had died away and the coffin was lowered, Mammy Fuller said to Mrs. Wilkie : " Ma, I don't know when I enjoyed anything so much. I have been near Heaven all the time."

Mammy Fuller knew that for Mary there had been an abundant entrance, and that we should sorrow not, for if we believe that Jesus died and rose again, even so them also which sleep in Jesus will God bring with Him.

Printed at the Press of the Publishers